Testimonial:

"Julie nails it! The best investment you will ever make is an investment in YOU, because who you are becoming is more important than what you do. The potential upside for a significant return on investment from utilizing this book is priceless! Get a PhD in YOU is just that - an investment in uncovering the best version of yourself, who is meant to shine and feel purposeful so you can live your most fulfilling life. I'm thrilled that Julie is sharing her strategies with the world and for the journey that you're about to embark on!"
Hal Elrod, #1 Bestselling Author, *The Miracle Morning* **(www.MiracleMorningBook.com)**

"Get a PhD in YOU is refreshingly honest and delivers a powerful punch of radical self-acceptance. Julie Reisler gracefully walks readers through fun and effective journal exercises to live each day with more passion, purpose, and pleasure. Her miraculous self-discovery workbook offers the guidance and inspiration you've been searching for—all substance, no fluff! Julie reminds us all of the importance of looking deep within, getting real with ourselves, and showing up big. Right now. You will feel focused, free, uplifted, and inspired to finally live your truth."
Kate Eckman, TV Presenter, Model, Motivational Speaker and Author

"Julie Reisler walks her talk. Her wisdom is derived not simply from knowing how to live a joyful life but authentically living one. Embodying unconditional self-love is easier said than done, and Julie's actionable daily practices make the mountain feel more like a molehill. Her gentle hand will guide your path, and her sparkle will help you find your own."
Danette Wolpert, Founder and Executive Director of the Illuminate Film Festival (www.illuminatefilmfestival.com)

"A practical yet profound approach to introspection. Julie perfectly captures what so many of us need to get our behinds in gear and to start creating the life that we know we are capable of. It's a perfect mix of food for thought and powerful exercises all delivered in a very relatable and genuine package. A fun and insightful read!"
Mark DeNicola, Writer & Director at Collective Evolution (www.collective-evolution.com) and Founder of Beam Beam Productions (www.beambeampictures.com)

"A book on creating the best YOU, you can be. Well done, Julie. When I first picked up Julie's book, I knew I was in for a treat. Julie gets it...if you are looking to tweak, fine tune and focus on developing a better you, don't miss out reading this book, *Get a PhD in YOU*. Be ready to take plenty of notes, because you are going to learn a lot about YOU!"
Doug Sandler, Mr. Nice Guy, Author and Speaker, #1 Best Seller on Amazon, *Nice Guys Finish First* **(www.dougsandler.com)**

"Beloved Julie, thank you. My appreciation to you for creating your beautiful self affirming workbook *Get a PhD in YOU*. Interwoven throughout your very impressive and most important creation BE innate sense of an ancient adage: Know Thyself. As we read your empowering words, what is absolute is an inspiring message of encouragement and love. Your self knowing is an exalting exhortation for Life. ~ You are revealing supportive self motivational sacredness, information allowing Humans to enjoy experiencing personalizing their potential while creating worthy works, accomplishing actions and deeds; and, mind you, fearlessly owning, utilizing their self knowledge experiences. Yes! You go, Girl. ~ Julie, you BE beneficent mentor presenting astute wisdom; because of your generosity, countless participants will acknowledge, accept and achieve some very qualifying results. *Get a PhD in YOU* is a vital and celebratory message, a wonder filled Testimony to Life and all Its radiant and remarkable Majesty. Thank You for extending Your spiritually significant message. Blessings Abundantly Deserved."
Reverent June Juliet Gatlin, Woman of Prophetic Vision, Inspiration and Song, Best Selling Author of Book, *Spirit Speaks To Sisters* **(www.reverentjunegatlin.com)**

"Julie's love for humanity and the ability we all have to design our lives is expressed in this transformative book. If you want to create a life with more freedom, this book is for you!"
Marcus "Bellringer" Bell, Entertainment Entrepreneur/Music Producer

"There is nobody I would trust more to help me dig deeper into my own self-awareness and self-love. Julie has truly walked the path of healing to rediscover her joy and she wants to share it with all of us. Her love is genuine and her enthusiasm is contagious. Julie is a gem and this book is going to change lives."
Connie Bowman, Actress/Yoga Teacher/Author, *Back to Happy*

"Julie shows you how to truly design a life you love through stories, reflection, and creativity. Learn how to get unstuck, practice self-care, and honor those baby steps along the way with this enthusiastic and experienced guide."
Kimberly Wilson, Author and Therapist (www.kimberlywilson.com)

"WOW! This book is as authentic, loving, inspiring, purposeful, magical and playful as Julie herself. Julie taps into the universal truth that each and every one of us has the potential to become our best and highest self in such a fun, relatable and workable way. Her own inner light and highest best self shines through each and every one of the pages. As a like-minded warrior for passion, purpose and fulfillment and as a fellow student of the ever-exciting personal growth journey of life, I love *Get a PHD in YOU*!"
Rachel Ellner Lebensohn, Founder of Seyopa #SeizeYourPassion!

"This style of discovery work is literally right on time! Julie's creative and compassionate approach to the challenge of self-healing is totally transformative. If everyone did this work, the planet would light up with joy!"
Heather Keller, RN, Integrative Yoga Therapist, WOW Coach and Holistic Healer

"*Get a PhD in YOU* is an invaluable tool for someone who is ready to live better, love harder, aim higher, and shine brighter. No matter where you are in life's journey, this book applies to you. If you think this book is not for you, it is absolutely for YOU. Julie gives us a practical and impactful way to do the inner work necessary so that we can separate from self-imposed limitations. For several years, Julie has been instrumental in our wellness program as an empowerment strategist, cultivating clients toward their health and fitness goals. By Julie elegantly infusing her inspiring wisdom and personality onto these pages, it gives me and my patients a tangible pathway to attain personal breakthroughs."
Betty Y. Wang, DO, MBA, Physician and Founder of the Body and Wellness Program at BW Primary Care

"Julie hit a grand slam!!! *Get a PHD in YOU* is a phenomenal guide which takes you on a journey of self-discovery. As an amazing Life Design coach, Julie Reisler engages the reader to go deeper within and discover their true purpose in life. This journey will help you increase self-trust, improve your self-awareness, gain clarity in your life, and master the most important person...YOU! While exploring this material, you will be touched by Julie's authenticity as she shares her own life struggles and provides you with step-by-step instructions on ways she was able to grow through adversity. Upon completing this workbook you will definitely have a much better relationship with YOU, the most important person there is!"
Eric Konovalov, CEO of The Goal Guide, Speaker, Trainer (www.thegoalguide.com)

"Julie is the kind of mentor you long for: kind, wise, authentic, and endlessly enthusiastic about your potential being revealed! Tired of being less than? Then grab this book and get ready to journey toward your greatness."
Melissa Wadsworth, Dream Coach and Author of Collective Manifestation
(www.collectivemanifestation.com)

"We all long for authenticity. What better way to find it than in ourselves and then radiate it out to the world. Julie Reisler guides you to do just that in her brilliant book, *Get a PhD in YOU*. Julie helps you get rid of the clutter in your head to help you find the beauty and passion that's already in you – the authentic you."
Leah Friedman, Professional Organizer and Owner of Raleigh Green Gables: Organize Your Life!
(www.raleighgreengables.com)

"As one committed to helping others become their personal and professional best, I found *Get a PhD in YOU* to be an extraordinary resource and guide to helping you uncover your potential and most extraordinary you. I'd highly recommend this book to anyone looking to transform their life from the inside out. Julie has clearly done the personal work on herself and shares her wisdom with her readers in how to design their best life. We all could use a PhD in YOU."
Debi Silber, MS, RD, WHC, FDN

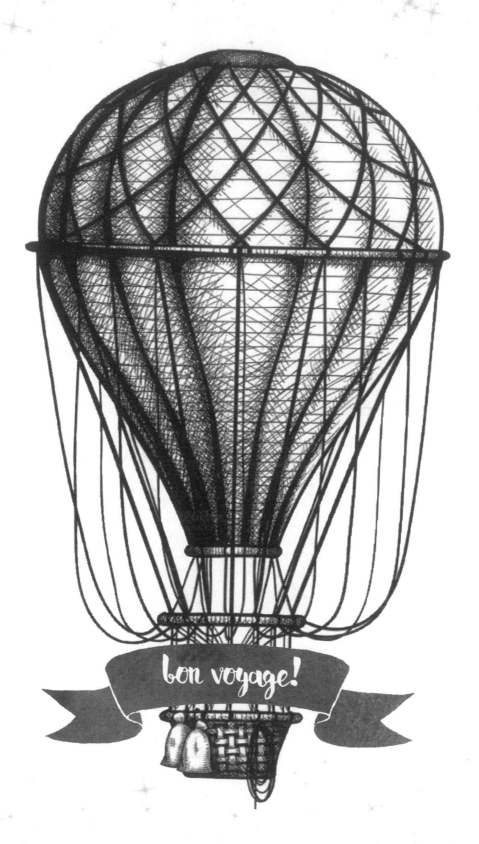

A Course in Miraculous Self-Discovery

GET A PHD

—— IN ——

You are the person you will spend the most time with.
Ever. Investing time, energy, and resources in yourself
will pay dividends beyond your wildest dreams.
Using Get a PhD in YOU, you can begin to excavate
the most extraordinary version of YOU.

JULIE REISLER

ISBN: 9780692795408
Cover Design by Catie Collins and Christy Jenkins
Interior Design by Christy Jenkins
Photo by Mary Gardella

Published by:
Empowered Living, LLC Books
1519 York Road
Lutherville, MD 21093

I dedicate this
to all of you who've been
blind to your inner magnificence.

May this help you
to discover and embrace
all of the brilliance
that is YOU.

"Create the highest, grandest vision possible
for your life, because you become what you believe."
~Oprah Winfrey

"You were born with everything
you need to answer the call of your soul."
~Marie Forleo

"So as you are beginning your day anchor yourself in the truth.
Know that all is well. Extend this to your friends, colleagues
and all that you meet That life is for YOU! It is never against you."
~Rev. Michael Bernard Beckwith

"To love ourselves and support each other in the process of becoming real
is perhaps the greatest single act of daring greatly."
~Brene Brown

Table of Contents

Acknowledgements

First, I want to thank my Creator (God, Higher Power, Divine Source Energy) for whispering in my ear to create this book and then providing all of the incredible people to help me along the writing trek. This book would not have been possible without the support, wisdom, love and belief that my many "teamsters" have in me.

I want to especially acknowledge my mom, Helene Reisler, who has been the quintessential model of love, positivity, and that all things are possible. To my Dad ("D"), Ron Reisler, for his unwavering support and a special shout out to my incredibly loving and stunning sister, Emily McAllister, an amazing writer, photographer, creative, DIYer, artist, singer, believer in me, and for always giving me a second chance and for helping me to be my best.

Thank you to my delicious children, Dalia and Ami. You are my constant teachers, reminding me what's really important in life and what it feels like to love beyond words. To their father, Asher, my co-parenting partner, thank you for giving me my two greatest gifts on the planet.

To my beautiful husband Heath, who has always had my back and encouraged me no matter what. Thank you for showing me what it means to be a phenomenal partner and printing my very first copy of *Get A PhD in YOU!* I am eternally grateful.

To my oldest and dearest friend since I was five years old, Meg Kassakian Connolly (who has her actual PhD in Psychology), my soul sister since we were in Mrs. D's first grade class, thank you for reminding me to always show up for my life and to do the work.

Paula D. Atkinson, lover of all beings, thank you for showing me what it looks like to love yourself and teaching me to be authentically me. Much of my growth and learning came from your unbelievable support.

With gratitude to all of the other incredible contributors to this book: Christine Brown — believing mirror and chief support team officer; Melissa Wadsworth — my magical manifesting editor; Amy Morris — my Sedona soul sista and editor extraordinaire; Christine Papadopolous — my first test reader and wise woman; Elena Hershey — my grammatical (Queen of Grammar) editor; Valerie Maguire — my honorary editor and dear confidant; Catie Collins — my incredibly creative and magnificent cover designer and pal; Christy Jenkins — my patient and brilliant book interior designer; Aunt Melyssa Cooke — for all your incredible ideas and comments; Leah Lakins — believer in me and Fresh Eyes editing skills; Neil Roseman and Phill Thomas — for your incredible coaching and personal development courses; and all the many friends who graciously supported me during this process. I am deeply grateful to my many dear supporting friends over the years who believed in me and helped me earn my PhD in ME: Lisa Regina, Adina Zarchan, Alisa Lebensohn, Phyllis Fagell, Karen Stern, Valerie Theberge, Shari Hammond, Megan McReynolds, Katie Kramer, Michelle Oullette, Randi B, Paige Rien, Karin Mitchell and Tamar Epstein. I am grateful to Jennifer Ransaw Smith, for encouraging me to step into my empowered self and write this book. A special thanks to Martie Pineda for showing me how to map out my book from a right brain perspective; Lisa Stearns for reviewing this baby for any oversights; Jenna Lamere for your creative genius support; and Emily Lodge, yoga teacher extraordinaire, for reminding me about rowing your own boat in her delicious yoga class. I'm honored to have studied the completion process with Teal Swan, renowned Spiritual Catalyst, and for Teal reminding me that I'm 'the bridge.' I am also profoundly thankful to my dear new friend, the deeply wise and divinely connected Reverent June Juliet Gatlin for encouraging me to move forward with my book and to stand my sacred ground.

I am eternally grateful to my Grandma Roslyn who has been with me in spirit, as well as, my other guides and angels.

Finally, dear readers, thank YOU for having the courage to work through this book and actualizing your soul purpose.

If I missed mentioning your name, you know who you are, and I am eternally grateful for your contribution.

"Row, row, row your boat.
Gently down the stream.
Merrily, merrily, merrily, merrily.
Life is but a dream.

~English Nursery Rhyme

Introduction

Hello, my new friend! I'm Julie Reisler, your guide and co-creator on your most important journey down the stream of self-discovery. I want to honor you, and applaud you, for making an empowered choice to really explore what your potential is and how you want to express that potential in the world.

Like this simple nursery rhyme says, life can be dream-like when you choose to row your own boat (not someone else's), with joy and merriment.

As a life design coach, I am passionate about changing lives. This book is my way of offering you a special space for growth. It is a safe place to return to as you journey through important and magical steps of self-discovery that lead to you being your whole beautiful self. In a world of distraction, this book reminds you that YOUR most important focus is yourself. It is your intentions, your progress, your dreams, and your ability to shine in the world that make the difference.

This book comes from listening to my intuition that insisted for a whole year that I create a book. That guiding voice didn't stop until I listened and took action. I've learned through my own self-discovery work that sharing authentically is the best way to make a real difference in others' lives. Simultaneously, this process helps me to become more attuned to my own humanity. I openly share about the parts of my life that weren't working for me. I share the tools and magical daily practices I used to change those circumstances. If there is anything you'd like to revamp in your own life, I will walk you through the process along with me. This is a win-win for both of us!

Trust that your intention, along with your intuition, will help direct you. Trust that your life is unfolding perfectly through your choices and actions, and that you will find the personal and career paths that are right for you.

We all have layers of comparative thinking and socialized beliefs that dull our true brilliance and radiance. This book is designed to help you strip away anything that dulls your light. By the end of this journey you will be seeing yourself and your purpose with more crystal-clear clarity. You will shine!

Make this a pivotal starting point

Less than a decade ago, I woke up in the middle of the night in a sheer panic. My agitated body was telling me that hiding behind the mask of a people-pleaser was no longer working for me. While quite scary, this wake-up call resulted in my embracing my true possibilities, power, and potential.

If you long to wake up to your own greatness, start here. Society gives you generalized measurements for success. I'm giving you tools to realize your true individual purpose and value. My purpose is to help you discover the seeds to your power and creative genius that lie within you. They won't be found outside of you. YOU hold the keys to your purpose and passion.

"Choose wisely. There are only two ways to live your life. One is as though nothing is a miracle. The other is though everything is a miracle."
~Albert Einstein

I recently read in a study that the chances of being born are 1 in 14 trillion. Now *that* feels like a miracle, like a huge opportunity. So how are you choosing to be your whole, alive miraculous self today?

The mere fact that you are inclined to learn more about how to nurture, honor, and develop YOU is something to acknowledge and celebrate right off the bat! You can't give to others what you don't have. It takes courage to look in the mirror and to understand that you are the common denominator in your life. I wholeheartedly believe that it pays off big time to research and study your life motivations, interests and dreams just like you'd pursue a PhD. The focus is YOU!

I walk my talk. I have found that by investing my own time, resources, energy, money, and emotions into learning more about me, there are massive payoffs, residual gifts, dividends, and even miracles that continue to come into my life. As my best friend Meg said to me during a very tough personal time, "You are going to stay stuck in the mud until you learn to get yourself out of it. You can't keep complaining and blaming—you have to do the work." She encouraged me to look at my part in a tough situation and how I contributed to my personal upset. I invite you to see from my stories what resonates with you. As I learned from my first support group, pay attention to what resonates and feel free to leave the rest!

My first 35 years of life taught me that I can't truly love myself until I have compassion for myself. This foundation of self-love and care is priceless. There is nothing money can buy that will provide the inner peace and genuine self-respect gleaned from doing my own inner work. Today, I honor and respect the darkest moments in my past knowing that they pointed the way to my most valuable life lessons. I share what has worked for me to help you illuminate your own infinite possibilities. I used to think of myself as a mediocre side dish; I just didn't have the right stuff to be a main dish (more about my relationship to food later). Now life is the most delicious and satisfying feast I ever dreamed of... and you, too, can have that!!

As you progress through this self-guided study of YOU, it is my hope you will embrace your journey of personal development as the very thing that unlocks your potential. This workbook is geared to stimulate you to dig deeper and become aware of your mental habits and patterns by bringing them into the light. Use the tools here that best support you in becoming who YOU want to be. I believe you can achieve a new kind of PhD, a "Doctorate of Possibility" for envisioning and creating the most fulfilling life you can imagine.

Changing the nature of your mind

In this book you engage in a journey of mental shifts. These shifts are to be nurtured in the soil of self-love and self-care. You'll start with honing your awareness, learning the importance of baby steps, and paying attention to how you fuel your body. You'll release the mental habits that no longer serve you as you create new narratives that inspire and nourish YOU. By the completion of this journey, you will have much more clarity around your purpose and your true capabilities. You'll see how purpose and passion show up in your day-to-day life. You'll choose your next steps forward. All this sets the stage for your beautiful self to live a more inspired life full of possibility.

My Grandma Roslyn always said, "You can't love things, only people." Further refining that, I'd like to add, "You can't truly love others without first loving yourself." I'm still a "loving self" work-in-process, as you probably are, too. Graced with new ways of thinking and my dedication to supporting you, it will be easier than you imagine to love yourself more deeply than you've ever known. Just by picking up this book, I know that you are ready to embark on this amazing self-led journey.

There is only one of YOU on this entire planet. Each of us is born with distinct interests and exceptional talents, possessing sacred gifts that are bestowed upon us. I know our world will benefit tremendously from your willingness to uncover YOU so you can share your voice, purpose, and greatness from your own unique perspective.

The planet desperately needs you to love and honor yourself fully so you can spread that throughout the rest of the world.

Welcome to your expanded life!

With love, light, & magic,
Julie

The universe pays you back
for taking risks on its behalf.

~Shakti Gawain

Investing in YOU

Ibelieve that YOU star in your life. To do this with consciousness, it is crucial that you understand your own individual way of starring in your life story. I now fully own the effects of owning my starring role in all of my interactions, communications, and relationships. It is crucial that we understand our own individual way of starring in our life stories. Otherwise, you can end up living life as a victim. For instance, my victimization came out in funky ways, such as being passive aggressive, manipulative, jealous, and disempowered. Since my default operating system is people pleasing, I would do everything in my power to have you like me, or failing that, find something wrong with you to make myself feel better. Either way I would often feel less than worthy, not good enough. While I knew I couldn't change others, my victimhood was so strong that it impacted the people in my world and caused them to treat me poorly. I believe that our attitudes and how we view the world greatly impacts how we view ourselves and those around us. Our way of being is contagious.

When I began to understand that my view of myself influenced how others treated me, I gained a powerful sense of responsibility for myself. This taught me I am the common denominator of all my thoughts and experiences and the steward of my own mind. When I got that being a victim didn't serve me, I had a massive mind shift and a beautiful breakthrough star was born. Remember, breakdowns and breakups always lead to breakthroughs.

How this journey began

The old me would have only wanted you to see the final package—the Julie that is always put together, appropriate, agreeable, eating the perfect diet, and saying and doing the "right" things. However, my protective self, the mask behind who I really am, slammed into a proverbial wall. I had an intense realization that living my life in the looking-perfect-lane had to come to a screeching halt.

Like many young girls, I was an active kid and obsessed with my body and weight. My mom offered me a buffet of after-school activities from ballet and gymnastics to piano lessons and swimming. Many of those activities required a tight swimsuit or leotard, which was definitely not my idea of fun. By any standard, I was crazy lucky to have these opportunities, experiences, and familial love. But all the external love and support couldn't give me what I needed the most — internal self-love and appreciation. Instead of self-worth I felt self-shame, and I began a long journey and vicious cycle of self-loathing.

My way of coping with this self-loathing was turning to food—using it like a favorite stuffed animal or a pacifier. I'm sure if you picked up this book, you can relate to those feelings of losing love for yourself or of never having developed it to begin with. I would choose to play with certain friends because of their stash of snacks and food. Often, I ate my sister's leftovers during dinner and then I would sneak three or four more helpings afterwards. I would steal candy from my dad's stash in the basement, where he hid bags of bulk candy from the rest of us. Worse yet, I would eat food out of the trash (yup) and pretend that it was totally normal to retrieve stale, half-eaten cookies from the garbage. I remember joining the ski team just so I could sell M&M's. Eighteen boxes later I realized that I ate almost a full case!

My only saving grace was my mother who encouraged me to look in the mirror each morning and repeat goofy affirmations around self-love. For those of you who grew up in the '90s like me, she was a lot like the character Stuart Smalley from *Saturday Night Live*. Little did I know how helpful, lifesaving, and life-giving this practice would become in my life. Thank you, Mom!

Mirror declarations are one of the easiest and most freely accessible ways to love yourself right NOW.

Now, thanks to studying the work of the incredible self-help guru Louise Hay who delves seriously into mirror work, I affirm my love and respect for myself in the mirror daily. Sometimes those affirmations make me chuckle. Yet most days I am full of deep gratitude, appreciation, and the hope that I can share and empower others to build that same kind of self-love. Of course, there are days when I want to turn away, but I know that even though this can be one of the hardest parts in the YOU PhD program, mirror work is one of the easiest and most freely accessible ways to love yourself.

Getting real

Getting real with myself was one of my most painful, yet important, life lessons. Using food to cope with my negative emotions, I gained and lost the same 40 pounds four different times. I secretly shoved down all my feelings, fears, worries, and even some dreams, with whatever sugary, fatty, or salty item I could find. I used food to deal with:

· my teenage-girl insecurities
· my parents' separation
· marrying and divorcing a great guy at a young age
· settling for secure jobs that didn't feed my insatiable hunger for self-worth

It wasn't until I binged on two pounds of M&Ms (definitely an unhealthy obsession) in a 15-minute sitting that I realized my life was heading into a serious danger zone. This binge left me sick for three days. Only then did I find a small kernel of willingness to start looking at what was really going on within me. Finally, I asked myself, "What was at the bottom of the emptiness I was trying to fill?"

I had enough hope to see that perhaps there was a way out of this so-called ideal life I was creating to cover up the absolute mess I felt inside. It was during this dark night of my soul that my world started to change. My internal light began to flicker ever so slightly. As with any change, many times my journey was painful, uncomfortable, disorienting, and frightening. Yet, I knew on the other side it would be exciting, intriguing, and laden with new possibility. After talking to a trusted mentor, I realized I needed to take action towards excavating the real me. At the intersection of my despair and optimism was an opening where endless possibilities could be birthed.

My first major step was deciding to attend a support group for compulsive overeaters. While I knew my bingeing was more than just about the food, I needed to address the physical health issue in order to be ready to grasp all of the wisdom and insights of this life challenge. It was the path that enabled a new mindset to develop. Twelve years later, I'm still on that journey, and it has produced some of the most incredible life changes. I now have the ability to practice being present and to choose listening to my inner voice. I've discovered this is a journey of being willing to be a beginner, endure discomfort, learn to fall (sometimes face down), open up to my humanity, and change my habits for the better. This has given me more inner peace than I ever could have imagined, not to mention the joy of being in service to others by sharing my experiences. Ripping off the societal layers of expectation and measurement, I woke up to my truth.

Vows to ourselves

When I became clear about my purpose and passion, part of which was to write and share my experience, I made an internal contract with myself—a promise—to wake up each morning with the willingness to show up for my life. While I didn't write a formal contract at the time, I did journal a lot about what I wanted to change, shift, create, and have happen in my life. I made a conscious decision to use all of my painful experiences and growth opportunities as a way to help others going through similar rough patches. My choice was to be authentic, vulnerable, and open to sharing my true self.

As I jump into my life, often I love what's showing up. Other times this path is hard, painful, uncomfortable, and quite tough. Yet, I have chosen to be present for all that occurs knowing that each time I move through a challenge or embrace a new opportunity, I am in action. I can't make changes without a willingness to change. With practice, I have learned to take on change with enthusiasm, excitement, courage, joy, and love. Before you enroll in the most important course of your lifetime —the study of YOU— I encourage you to sign this contract with, and for, yourself. **I have provided a sample on page 159, or you can create your own. The important thing is to DO IT!**

Make a copy and post it somewhere you will see it every day. I wish for you all the courage, insight, wisdom, curiosity, intrigue, vulnerability, and awareness that you long for on your journey. I want you to realize that you already have

The YOU Contract

I _____, a precious, one-of-a-kind, incredible human being, promise to embrace my humanity to the best of my ability. I promise to show up for my life at all times. I know there will be moments and days where I have no desire to be present or engage in my current life situation. In these moments I will commit to honoring, caring, nurturing, and loving myself even more. I will not let one situation, experience, or limited thought get in my way. I agree to toss the word "perfect" out of the window, as I know it doesn't exist and will only keep me playing small.

As I start showing up for all of my life, my life will begin to open up, transform, and become outrageously delicious beyond my wildest imagination. With each experience, I am open to learning, growing, and gaining new perspectives.

I am willing and ready to take on the study and the wonder of me. I will be as serious and devoted to the study of me as I would in any graduate or certification program. I will devote the necessary time, intention, attention, and curiosity needed for me. I am open to life's abundance, gifts, insights, and joy so that I can unleash my best self. I am here, I am committed to taking action, and I'm game. I am willing to love and care for all of me — mind, body and spirit.

_____   _____
Name   Date

Have fun here, my friend.
Draw your own personalized logo or symbol:

EVERYTHING you need and want inside of YOU. Have fun, be daring, be brave, and know that you are embarking on a magical path that I promise will lead to an even more incredible you.

Get ready for an amazing adventure and please share with others how life is opening up to your wildest possibilities! Don't forget to share new openings and insights with me, too, at www.juliereisler.com. We can all use more positive personal stories. If you'll allow me, I'd like to be a trusted mentor for you.

After talking to a trusted mentor, I realized I needed to take action towards excavating the real me. This is where my despair met my optimism and birthed my faith. — Julie Reisler

Chapter 1 Tap-into-You Journal Space

Provided for you throughout this workbook is journal space to use on a daily, bi-weekly, or weekly basis. Use it to reflect on your feelings and insights related to the chapter topic you have just covered.

Have fun with this journal writing. If a little stuck, I highly suggest getting out colored pencils or crayons and begin by coloring on your journal page. Did you know that coloring and drawing helps you to tap into your creativity, thoughts, and beliefs? And it can be super fun. We are all creative beings, so just let go and let it flow. When you feel that you have relaxed into that space for yourself, begin writing (and if you want, keep drawing).

Related to this chapter, think about the following: What have I learned about the importance of investing in myself? Why? What changes am I committed to working on throughout this workbook? What will I do to keep myself committed on a regular basis? Maybe set daily time to dedicate to myself?

WRITING PROMPT: If you want some help focusing on what you learned in this chapter, you can use these writing prompts at the end of each chapter as a starting point. Simply write the prompt and then complete the sentence. Try not to lift your pen from the paper; keep the flow going. If you pause or feel stuck, simply write the prompt again and complete it again. Try this at least for a few minutes. It's a good practice for getting out of your everyday mental mind and tapping into expanded knowing

journal

TAP INTO YOU

space

"I define (or see) my value as . . ."

"Happiness is not something ready-made. It comes from your own actions."

~ Dalai Lama

Research and Reflection

I often hear a lot of my clients take an exasperated breath when we start talking about doing work on themselves. I see eyes widening, sighs of frustration, a look of fear, serious concern, and often anxiety that life is about to get hard. The reason I know I'm meant to coach and guide people in these moments is because I actually welcome and embrace this encounter. This is where you get to really start playing with your beliefs, thoughts, words, and the lenses you use to view your own life. What if you could pause, take a breath, and choose to see doing the work as a voyage? This is the sweet spot of change on its way. It's like turning the corner on the highway of hope. You're about to see a vista that you have never viewed before.

This is the sweet spot of change on its way. It's like turning the corner on the highway of hope. You're about to see a vista that you have never viewed before.

Start your research and reflection

Here's an even better analogy: scientists are trained to do research. In order to come up with findings to a hypothesis, they have to first do their research. As you embark on your quest of knowing and honoring yourself in order to make change, it's going to take research, time, growth experiences, and lots of nurturing. Change takes patience, practice, pace, and persistence. It's important to start reflecting on how you really feel about yourself and the internal messages you generate. The following exercises are inspired by my own inner transformation to self-love.

I first became aware of the idea of using a mirror as part of feeling and generating self-love through personal growth teacher and author Louise Hay. Mirror work, as Louise Hay coins it, is essentially the practice of deeply looking at oneself in the mirror and repeating personal affirmations and messages of self-love.

How do you actually feel about yourself when you look in the mirror? We do it everyday, all the time, be it in an actual mirror or perhaps in the reflection of a store window or in someone else's sunglasses (yup — I've done that too and it's totally human). To gauge where you are on the self-love spectrum, just think of your self-love capacity like a gas tank that is somewhere between empty and full. How full is your self-love tank?

Begin by looking at yourself (in the mirror or, if you're not ready for that, look at a photograph of yourself, etc.). What do you notice? What do you feel about the person looking back into your eyes? Are you feeling connected or as though you haven't really seen your own self for years? Do you want to cry? Look away? Feeling a tad uncomfy with this practice? Just notice, while trying to do so without judgment. Most days I am able to stare at my own eyes, blow a kiss back to myself, and know that I'm a special divine creature because I'm alive, kickin' and here to say that out loud. On good days I even feel this in my bones. On other days, I respond to myself with a less-than-kind remark. When that happens, I know I need to sit with the discomfort of not feeling enough or loving myself fully. At these moments I ask myself, "How can I love myself more today so I have more to give others?" or "How can I connect with my higher self, the internal aspect of me that has a divine right to be on the planet?" The physical mirror becomes a pathway connecting my surface self to my true inner self. This practice affirms that all healing, happiness, and peace is created out of love.

The point here is to build a relationship with yourself. I've found that learning to truly connect with myself has worked brilliantly with the mirror. Wherever you are along the spectrum of self-love and connection is perfectly fine. It's information as to how you view yourself — literally — and how you feel about your reflection.

Illuminate Your Inner and Outer Selves

My intention is to strengthen your relationship between your inner and outer reflections. If you're noticing that you want to turn away, laugh, or do anything but this exercise, it's a good idea to start with connecting to your inner self. I've outlined below ways to do this. Start with your gifts and what you appreciate about yourself. Nurture and acknowledge your inner self first until you feel grounded, connected, and comfortable looking in the mirror while recognizing them.

Here are 3 reflection practices that help connect you to your whole glorious self:

1. **Personal Bests Practice.** List one area of interest you're naturally good at and one personal quality you love about yourself (if this feels fun, list 2, 3, or as many as you'd like).

Your natural interests and the natural qualities of your personality are how you develop and express your most authentic self to the world. Most of us forget the natural gifts we have and use every day to be of service to others and create a life filled with satisfaction. Focus on your gifts and qualities for at least a minute. Allow appreciation, gratitude, or whatever feeling comes up to flow and circulate like golden light through your body and mind.

2. **Strength-Divining Practice**. Reflect on your outer and inner strengths. Look into the mirror, embracing and acknowledging what you were born with as a strength (perhaps something like physical stamina or vocal abilities or something less obvious like your ability to laugh at yourself which makes others laugh, too). Consider what strengths you have developed over the years. This might be traits like resilience, persistence, compassion, self-honesty, or empathetic listening. Feel the beauty and power of your outer and inner strengths for 15 seconds. Build to 30 seconds, 45 seconds, and eventually 1 minute. It might feel weird at first and that is ok. It's very normal to shift back and forth from acceptance to judgment. Our minds are designed to generate chatter and to compare. Work on connecting back to your highest self, the YOU that exists and has nothing to do with appearances or what others deem important. Notice what it feels like in your body to acknowledge your strengths. Notice anything different in your eyes or face as you consider your strengths? Maybe you don't notice anything but you feel a warmth in your chest or uplifting in your spirit. **Note what you feel.** This is an indication of your increased connection to the essence of you.

3. **Loving Looks Practice.** Once you feel solid in your ability to look at the mirror and focus on yourself, you might decide to try holding your attention on specific parts of your body. What do you see that you can appreciate? Start with your eyes. Notice the black of your pupil. Embrace the outer color of your eyes. What might they be saying to you? Can you appreciate your eyes as the beholder of all your life experience? Can you find appreciation in having eyes in the first place? Look at your

lips. Focus on the shape, creases, color and outline. You took your first breath with these lips, and nourishment and speech flow through these lips. How does it feel to connect more intimately with your eyes, lips and perhaps rest of your face?

Note what is it like to focus on your appearance with appreciation vs. judgment? What other part of your body could use some love and attention so that you feel like the whole package?

Society creates false standards of beauty and success. When you break from falsely trying to identity with, or compare yourself, to these standards you open yourself to the fuller expression of your true essence.

Daily Magical Practices #1: YOU Declarations

It takes practice to get comfortable with really connecting to YOU and your love for your amazing self. I know this because I practice it daily.

This is a world-changing love investment in YOU. The more we invest in loving ourselves as our unique, authentic, and incredible selves, the more goodness we can give to one another and ultimately to our family, friends, communities, nations, and planet. Making a difference and giving of ourselves to others is one of the most rewarding gifts. In order to love anyone else, we must learn first how to love ourselves. When we take any step forward towards actualizing our best selves, the Universe (God, Higher Power, Divine Goddess, Mother Earth, Source Energy, etc.) always rewards us.

Getting comfy with reflection and declaration time

What you say to yourself impacts how you feel and what you believe. This is a practice that develops clear intention. It allows you to pay attention to the words you choose and how those words make you feel. Want to change how you talk to yourself? Try at least one of these declarations every day. Pick and choose the affirmations that resonate with you. Change it up so you are really hearing it and feeling it. Many of my declarations have been inspired by Louise Hay's Mirror Work affirmations. If these words don't feel good, create ones that speak to YOU.

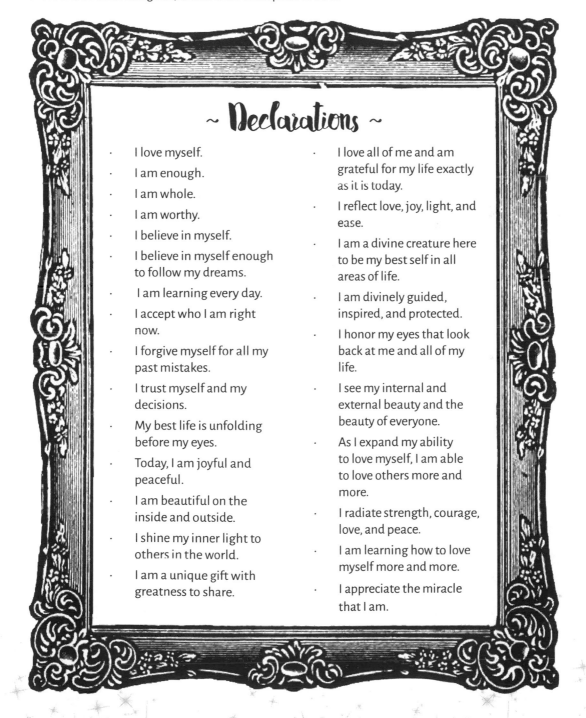

~ Declarations ~

- I love myself.
- I am enough.
- I am whole.
- I am worthy.
- I believe in myself.
- I believe in myself enough to follow my dreams.
- I am learning every day.
- I accept who I am right now.
- I forgive myself for all my past mistakes.
- I trust myself and my decisions.
- My best life is unfolding before my eyes.
- Today, I am joyful and peaceful.
- I am beautiful on the inside and outside.
- I shine my inner light to others in the world.
- I am a unique gift with greatness to share.
- I love all of me and am grateful for my life exactly as it is today.
- I reflect love, joy, light, and ease.
- I am a divine creature here to be my best self in all areas of life.
- I am divinely guided, inspired, and protected.
- I honor my eyes that look back at me and all of my life.
- I see my internal and external beauty and the beauty of everyone.
- As I expand my ability to love myself, I am able to love others more and more.
- I radiate strength, courage, love, and peace.
- I am learning how to love myself more and more.
- I appreciate the miracle that I am.

Your turn. Take a stab at it. **Try writing your own YOU affirmative declarations.**

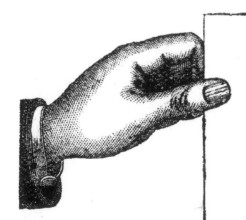

Reminder: You must master a
new way to think before you
can master a new way to be.
~Marianne Williamson

Creative Activity: Daily Mirror Magic

I'm a creativity appreciator and believe in the power of affirming through action. When I work with clients, I often combine the practice of mirror declarations with the action of creating one's own Magic Mirror!

Yep, we're talking about getting crafty here, friends! You are going to make your very own Self-Lovin' Mirror Magic!

The goal here is to get creative and have fun!

Here's what you'll need:
- A handheld mirror (easy to find and inexpensive at a local drug store)
- Glue
- Glitter
- Scissors
- Ribbon, feathers, beads, stickers, fabric (anything you want for decorating—as elaborate or as simple as you desire)
- Indelible markers (such as black, various rainbow colors, and metallic colors like gold or silver)
- Favorite statement or words related to what you'd like to be reminded of when you look in the mirror

Statement examples:
- Beauty comes first from within
- Be You; Everyone else is taken
- I am beautiful on the inside and out
- I radiate light, love, and peace

Affirmative word examples:
- courage
- strength
- light
- love
- wisdom
- beauty
- joy
- peace
- truth
- kindness

Step 1. Arrange all your goodies on a table. Light a gorgeous candle, put on your fave chill music (some of my favorites are the Wailin' Jennies, James Taylor, and Allison Krauss), and you're ready to make your very own Magic Mirror.

Step 2. Decorate the back of the mirror with fabrics, glitter, stickers, words, or whatever floats your boat. I love the idea of writing a quote around the interior (reflective side) of the mirror, and perhaps adding a word or two that inspires you. This is going to be your Self-Lovin' mirror to use daily, so let your imagination go wild.

Step 3. Use your mirror daily to see the best in yourself by reflecting on your true, whole beauty inside and out. Let your Magic Mirror be a tool that helps fill up your self-love tank when you are feeling low.

The inspiration for this activity came from my dear friends and sisters, Tamar and Elana—two incredibly creative, loving, and inspirational badass women. Thank you, beautiful ladies!

Make it a Daily Habit

Saying the phrase "I love myself" or looking at yourself and repeating "I'm learning to love everything about me internally and externally" has enormous benefits. By doing Mirror Magic every day, you are recreating your truth to be one of self-love. This belief about yourself was not formed overnight, and it will not shift overnight. Change in habit of thought takes time.

I also want you to start practicing saying declarations to yourself using any mirror you come across. Remember, others have no friggin' idea what you are saying to yourself in your head. Thankfully we can't hear one another's inner monologue. I often wink at myself, which reminds me I have eyes to wink with and that life is meant to be joyful and fun.

Let's say you had a rough conversation with your boss. Use your mirror to remind yourself of how loved you are. Maybe you're feeling less-than or in a hyper-comparative mode? Go to the bathroom, lock the door and soothe yourself with loving words as you gaze into your mirror. You are learning to give yourself what you need. Yay you!

Changing how you literally see yourself starts with being a reflection of those desired changes during mirror play. You reflect back to yourself your inner light and divinity. This is a gift to YOU and to others because you will continue to reflect that to the planet.

"What if we could pause, take a breath,
and choose to see doing the work as a voyage?
This is the sweet spot of change on its way."
-Julie Reisler

Chapter 2 Tap-into-You Journal Space

This chapter emphasized the power of words, both spoken aloud and internally to yourself as inner dialogue. Use this chapter's journaling pages to play with using words that light you up. Note how your mirror practice is going and what activities helped you to discover more about yourself.

journal

TAP INTO YOU

space

"I am beginning to take charge of creating the life I want by..."

"Awareness is like the sun.
When it shines on things,
they are transformed."

-Thich Nhat Hanh

Without Awareness You're in the Dark

Time to get YOU out of the dark and into the light! Once I saw that there was another way to view life and myself through a new pair of lenses, I received the gift of awareness. Without awareness I would have remained stuck. My M&M binge became an ultimate gift in re-creating my life. Was it fun? No way, José! But that experience was crucial to my growth and transformation. Let's explore together how your difficult moments can lead to new awareness that guides your life. Strap on your seatbelt and get ready to view your life in a new way!

Sift for the gift

AWARENESS ACTIVITY ONE

1.   Look back at the last five to ten years of your life and jot down three positive awareness moments that came from tough situations.

2.   Now look a bit closer and write down the upsetting event(s) that preceded your new awareness.

3. Can you see a link to how breakdowns create breakthroughs? Jot down how these experiences could be perceived as gifts.

Did you notice during this activity that new awareness surfaces from a hard experience? In the past, you might have allowed that uncomfortable or upsetting situation to keep you in a victim mentality. But now, you can see that something in that experience allowed you to open your mind to a new perspective. Being open, even to a small degree, to greater understanding allows you to perceive the situation differently. **Train yourself to ask, "How can I learn from this experience?" This will always lead to new awareness, learning, and growth.** This kind of openness creates a much different experience than complaining, "Why does this always happen to me?" or "When will I find the right person?" In other words, you're learning to sift for the gift.

Now let's dig a little deeper with the next awareness activity.

AWARENESS ACTIVITY TWO

1. **Choose one of your three examples from the first activity.**

2. **Take a closer look and notice the point where something switched in your mind. What light went on bringing you new awareness?** *(For example, even after eating hundreds of M&Ms, I heard a small voice from within say, "You need help. You don't fully love who you are and there is the possibility of change." What did/does your inner voice say? I didn't quite know then how to shift away from using food to cope with my rocky emotions. However, I trusted I would find an answer to help me change my behavior. It was too painful to continue on as I was, and I was ready to choose differently.)*

3. Ask yourself: "Where in my life can I be more open to change?"

4. Some other great awareness-provoking questions include the following:

How can I learn something from this situation?

How can I honor my inner voice more?

What do I need to see that will help me shift my perspective?

What is it that I really need right now?

What might be the gift here?

Redefining self-work

In the previous 2 chapters, you have started to uncover the importance of being open and willing to receive your breakthrough moments. This is what I mean by doing self-work. Sometimes when I'm coaching my clients, I get slight pushback around doing more self-work. It can feel overwhelming, unmanageable, and never ending. I totally get this as I have been there many times myself.

Before I invite you further into this journey, let me redefine the word "work." Here's the thing — you can choose to view your inner work as drudgery, as a nuisance. Or you can choose to see it in a new way. What if you pretended you were a highly specialized scientist on a quest to learn about the inner workings of your life? Instead of getting attached to judging life's events, you could think about this self-discovery process like any scientific exploration. You have your hypothesis, observations, outcomes, summary, and key learnings. The important thing is to pinpoint your own exciting way to view life from a fresh vantage point. Be creative and think expansively.

How else can you reframe doing YOU-work so that it actually occurs for you as exciting, intriguing, or even thrilling?

I sometimes imagine my self-work as putting on a new pair of glasses with super clear lenses in a bedazzled frame, with a big peace sign and smiley face in the corners. My super seeing-the-light glasses allow me to see my personal growth as an amazing adventure. You can train yourself to find joy in spending your own precious time to start reflecting on your life's events—without judgment. We are programmed as humans to see something initially from a negative standpoint or bias. However, this can be changed as you learn to create new thought patterns and habits. Perhaps a more fun way to engage here is to think of it as your enthusiastic commitment to yourself vs. grueling work. You will look more closely at the power of words in Chapter 6.

Self-work also means showing up for yourself. Maybe this looks like booking a weekly "me only" date by going window shopping or walking through your local farm stand. Other forms of self-work could be journaling, meditating, finding an accountability partner, or making monthly collages. If you are committed to being a lifelong learner, your work becomes play.

If you're like me, a Type A overachiever, lifelong self-work might feel a little daunting, like an interruption to the life you want to be living. Here's what I've discovered — life lessons don't keep starting at zero. You get to build upon each new level of awareness and learn from your "mistakes." Ultimately I believe mistakes are necessary and our biggest teachers. The more we see life as a classroom, the more likely we are to play, try new things, be curious, be in action, and be open to asking ourselves new and loving questions.

Time for teamsters

Beware—you are going to start noticing a lot more about yourself, even some stuff you'd rather not see. Perhaps in the past, you felt it was too painful to really look at how you treat others, or worse, how you treat yourself. These blinders served you at one point. As you take them off, it's crucial to do so with love, respect, and compassion.

As human beings, we all have a blind spot we'd like to change. By default, we are designed as dynamic social beings to do the best we can with what resources we have. I have learned, with practice and time, to honor my blinders when they pop up. Remember, as a people pleaser, I sometimes go into a situation first seeing how I can make sure the person likes me, rather than getting grounded in what might be best for the situation. Without awareness, I wouldn't have even seen my people-pleaser blinders in the first place.

Word to the wise—don't go on this journey alone. Research shows that we flourish and feel more supported and connected when we authentically connect with others. Start asking yourself, "Who is on my team?" or, "Who can I share myself and my learnings with in a safe space?" It's okay and highly advisable to seek out coaches, mentors, accountability partners, or friends to support you along the way.

I believe that finding a select few people to cheer you on and discuss what you're seeing about yourself is imperative. Not only is it helpful to hear your thoughts reflected back, but it's also eye-opening to hear another's perspective and perhaps allow for them to see a blind spot you didn't know was there. These folks will become your esteemed team members. They are taking a stand in support of you becoming your best version of YOU.

Note: If there is a particularly tough area of your life where you are struggling with an addiction (e.g., food, alcohol, gaming, or drugs) there are many 12-step programs that offer free and incredible group support. You can find a sponsor and meet others who have had similar struggles and have prevailed.

Now, let's look at building your team!

Creating your YOU team
(Hint: Have fun here!)

1. List up to five friends or family members who have your back and would be thrilled to be on your team.

2. Name your team:

    a.   Create a mascot or identity:

    b.   Give your team a logo and tagline:

    c.   Create a mission statement:

3. Create positions for your team, such as president, CEO, cheerleader, director of marketing YOU, an accountability partner, or a celebration committee.

Position/Person: _____

Position/Person: _____

Position/Person: _____

Position/Person: _____

Position/Person: _____

4. Volunteer yourself on someone else's team!

People love to feel needed and helpful. Asking your loved ones to be on your team is allowing them to give back. You can also offer to help them create a team of their own and volunteer to be their first member. Remember, you get to design your life. By designing a team, you are ensuring that you will be supported to grow, learn, see the world in new ways, and increase your self-awareness.

When you have a solid foundation of honoring and loving your inner self, you are in a position to help others by modeling authenticity and wholeness. That's how you make a difference and spread compassion. Doing self-work can be an amazing life adventure full of growth, joy, and fun. I promise, it is worth your efforts and investment.

"Bless all your breakdowns, dips, doubts and U-turns, for without them there would be no growth. Growth leads to understanding, understanding leads to new actions, new actions lead to new habits, and new habits lead to inner peace." -Julie Reisler

Chapter 3 Tap-into-You Journal Space

Journal here what you have learned about the importance of self-awareness. How has changing your perspective changed your outlook in the past? How does attitude affect your ability to fulfill your dreams?

journal

TAP INTO YOU

space

"More than anyone _____ (person's name)

inspires me because . . ."

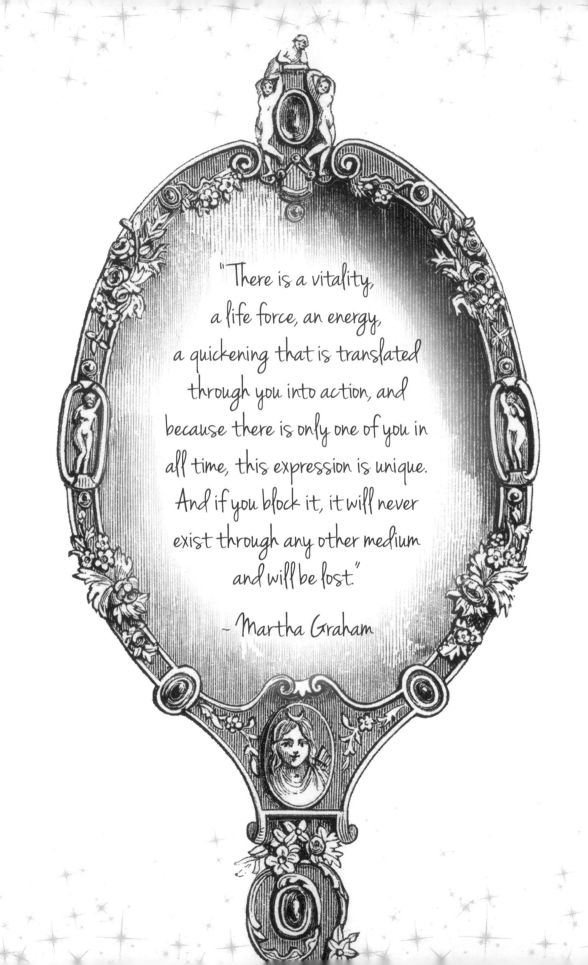

"There is a vitality,
a life force, an energy,
a quickening that is translated
through you into action, and
because there is only one of you in
all time, this expression is unique.
And if you block it, it will never
exist through any other medium
and will be lost."

~ Martha Graham

Releasing Fears So YOU Fully Show Up!

I learned a great lesson years ago: "I can't get much of anything if I don't show up for my life." Turns out that this growth lesson was the light at the end of a long, dark tunnel of feeling not-good-enough.

Part of this book is to help you discover your purpose, values, and gifts as well as to uncover what stops you from expressing these. It is my belief that we all arrive with divinely-inspired talents to use on this planet. To not show up, which translates into not using our gifts, would be a waste.

I went through a period both in my high school years, and again in my 20's, in which I was playing and living small. These were dark times. I stopped hanging out with my friends, withdrew from socializing, and used sugary and starchy foods to deal with my feelings of inadequacy. As a natural extrovert, this behavior was confusing, disturbing, upsetting, and caused me quite a bit of emotional turmoil and sadness. I stopped showing up for my life because I believed that I wasn't good enough to go out on Friday nights with friends or smart enough to converse with the super smart and popular kids.

Eventually, I learned the hard way that by not going to an audition, meeting, party or girls' night out, I was missing out on connecting with others and being present for life's surprises. I'm not going to lie; every now and then, my small "less-than" gal still shows up and I have to remind myself that she is based on old stories, tapes, and very limited beliefs.

I am encouraging you to tap and tune into your body and spirit to see where there might be something new to try, regardless of how scary or impossible it seems. As Lee Ann Womack sings in her song, "I Hope You'll Dance," my hope for you is that you see the value in going out on a limb. I hope you'll get your butt out there on the dance floor and shake it, gosh darn it! The more we practice any habit or thought pattern, the more comfortable it gets. Just like getting yourself to the gym, it's time to give your vulnerability muscle a workout.

What makes you feel inadequate? When do you catch yourself behaving less-than?

What does your less-than voice say to you at such times?

What fears stop you?

Fear is a fascinating emotion. It can stop you dead in your tracks or be the light under your butt that gets you to move into action. Fear can feel like a foggy daze that takes over your entire way of being or gives you permission to avoid participating in what you love to do. I've certainly been there. It can paralyze and overwhelm you, and certainly cause incredible amounts of stress.

I want to add that we are meant to have a range of emotions, fear being one of them. It's ok to have fear, and often it's an indication that there's something important to address within yourself.

My fears are generally based in not-good-enough thinking. You may withhold your light or play small for another reason. Some people have specific fears like a fear of speaking in public, that is based on a fear of "being seen." Others have fears based in something an adult or authority figure once said to them like, "You're not very smart," or "You aren't coordinated enough to dance." This can cause a feeling of overwhelm when you are presented with a situation in which you fear your so-called weakness will be found out. This might cause a fear of being vulnerable, or a fear of being shamed.

When I'm feeling overwhelmed with fear, I use a few basic techniques that help me to pause, re-center, and shift.

I typically first notice fear in my body. Fear and overwhelm show up as a tight and constricted feeling in my chest and a nauseous gut. That is the first clue I'm in the land of fear. What I do next is to pause and breathe. I literally stop and breathe deeply in my belly. Sometimes I'll put a hand on my heart and the other hand on my stomach. It's a love trick I've learned that helps me to remember to send love to myself and to breathe deeper through my diaphragm.

My next step is to take a mountain-top perspective. I'll imagine myself on the top of a gorgeous mountain in the Rockies (my future dream home) looking out at the landscape. From this vantage point, everything looks smaller and less overwhelming. I think about how whatever it is that's causing me the fear probably won't be in my consciousness in the next month, week, or even day. I also often ask myself, "When I'm 96, am I going to remember this incident? What do I want to look back and feel?" Once I start to get a more expansive view point, I then might look at when I've taken leaps of courage before and how that turned out (here's where looking at all life experiences as growth has become an asset). I also look at what I'm committed to in life – what are my core values? My values of love, courage, authenticity, of living life intentionally with purpose, and being of service and making a difference with others' help to guide me, act as pillars when I'm scared, insecure, struggling with overwhelm or the not-enough syndrome.

When you see fear-based thinking in a friend, it may be easy to realize the nonsense of it. You can see their loving gifts and potential waiting to emerge behind the fear. It can be harder to see it and shift it in ourselves. So here's your chance.

Let's do your fear inventory and assessment, shall we?

1. Write down 5 things that scare the heck out of you, and why:

2. Finish the following sentences:
"Because of fear, I have passed up on ..."

"If I felt no fear, the most outrageous thing I would try is ..."

"With no fear in sight, I'd take on ..."

"I'm going to start treating fear as an ordinary four-letter word and overcome my tendency to think small in regards to ..."

"Thank you, Fear, for trying to keep me safe, but this week I'm determined to start ..."

"Bye-bye, Fear! Thanks for what you taught me, but it's now time to take a different path. I'm now going to see myself as ..."

Tackling your fears

Our bodies are so smart. The more you practice locating fear, sadness, anxiety, anger, resentment, peace, or excitement, the more you will be able to use your body as a GPS. As I mentioned earlier, I sometimes know how I feel first through my body. I might be nervous about a presentation and not realize it until I notice that my chest feels a little tight or my stomach feels jumpy. Your body sensations are your own personal guide to gauging what's going on emotionally. Developing self-awareness and consciousness around how emotions are experienced by your body is worthwhile. It's like going on a treasure hunt in your own body. Discovering and describing your bodily sensations will give you great information.

Name a fear: _____

Does it have a color?

Does it have an identity or an avatar?

What does it look like?

Where do you feel this fear in your body?

What is your fear telling you?

Another great acronym I love is F.E.A.R. or False Evidence Appearing Real. We believe what our fear avatar tells us until we become aware that we are not our fears. My fear persona, whom I named Annie (no offense if this is your actual name), is this little shaky voiced thang that wears dark colors, hangs out on the couch all day in the dark, and is constantly looking for spiders and avoiding anything that feels out of her comfort zone. I sometimes have to calm her down and remind her that I'm safe and that it's okay to venture out and try big new projects like this book!

Once you become more aware, you can address your fears or anxiety with a new perspective. C. Joy Bell offers a refreshing perspective on fear: "Don't be afraid of your fears. They're not there to scare you. They're there to let you know that something is worth it."

You can feel fear and act anyway. As Eleanor Roosevelt once said, "Do one thing every day that scares you." Sage advice!

Here are some questions designed to help you see your thought and action patterns around fear:

1. When in your life were you scared to do something, but you moved through your fear and prevailed?

2. Recall an incident or time in which you have held back because of fear and doubt. (This one is not meant to make you feel badly or judge yourself. This is for research.)

3. Is there something right now in your life you really want? What is it?

4. What are your thoughts you tell yourself about making this happen?

5. What new supporting thoughts might you need or want to create to help you get what you want?

Are YOU showing up?

One of the most invigorating and pivotal moments for me was when I got crystal clear about taking on my life with purpose, and I chose to show up for my life, no matter what that looks like. Part of this was getting intentional about how to spend my time. Part of this involved confronting an old pattern of always doing for loved ones before considering self. I had to stay aware and keep choosing to change this pattern.

As humans who grow through experience, we are allowed to try new areas of interest. It helps if we give ourselves permission to make mistakes and play full out. **What I've learned is that giving my 100% doesn't look the same each day.** The most important thing for me is to be authentic and remain open to new ideas. The rewards for approaching life this way are both priceless and immeasurable. So many amazing people, opportunities, and gifts have landed in my lap because I was willing to imperfectly take that next step.

Writing this book has been all about feeling vulnerable AND showing up as my brightest-light self. If I had listened to all the many voices in my head about why I am not qualified to write a book, then this project would never have happened.

My old mental soundtrack around writing goes something like this:
· "Who are you to write a book? You never were very good at writing papers."
· You have too many thoughts at once and can't focus."
· "Your writing style is too flowery."
· "You take 100 words to say a simple thought."
· "Your communication style is better suited to a PA system!"

Sound familiar? Relate to this at all?

Over many years, and with the writing of this book, I have learned to turn down the volume on this soundtrack with practice, practice, practice, and more practice. I have realized that when I'm crazy passionate about a topic and can picture whom I am actually speaking to, I am a passionate writer.

The other thing that has made a big difference has been that for the past year, I have chosen to listen to my intuition instead, that small whisper telling me to write down my thoughts about what I've learned and gleaned from all of my own dark nights, breakdowns, U-turns, upsets, stuck moments, and pits of despair. I felt guided to write this workbook because I want to share what I have been blessed to learn.

I feel there is immense importance in sharing my experiences, hopes, and lessons learned — all in service of hopefully making an impact on YOU and your life. It is my dream to help you discover your greatness, fall in love with your fabulous self, and if you're stuck or feeling confined in your own thoughts, get un-stuck, and see that anything you want to create is possible. It is my hope that even if you have one major take away or *Ah-ha!* moment that positively affects your life, then I'm darn psyched and grateful to share myself and be of service.

I would be remiss if I didn't share the essence of this beautiful quote from Marianne Williamson's book, *A Course in Miracles*, that guides me all the time.

"Our deepest fear is not that we are inadequate. Our deepest fear is that we are powerful beyond measure. It is our light, not our darkness that most frightens us. We ask ourselves, who am I to be brilliant, gorgeous, talented, and fabulous? Actually, who are you not to be? Your playing small does not serve the world. There is nothing enlightened about shrinking so that other people won't feel insecure around you. We are all meant to shine, as children do. As we let our own light shine, we unconsciously give other people permission to do the same. As we are liberated from our own fear, our presence automatically liberates others."

Another thought that helps me daily is the belief that I choose to be brave, expose the real me, and show up with compassion, faith, and love, trusting my life will continue to be more delicious with miracles waiting to bud. I keep Shakti Gawain's quote over my bedroom loft that says, "The universe pays us back for taking risks on its behalf."

What risks are you willing to take? What risks must you take to fully be you or to get unstuck? As one of my favorite "lover of all beings," Paula, says, "Risk and you shall receive."

This is a good time to pause and take inventory. Let's get ready, get set, and let's get going!

1. *What does your highest-self want?*

2. *What new stories are needed now to support you taking a next step toward this goal?*

3. *What new affirmations can you create to support you?*

4. *How might you celebrate your courage and bravery in being the best you?*

It's easy to overlook that last step but it's crucial to honor ourselves as we grow.

Try doing something that really frightens you or makes you squirm. Just like any muscle that needs conditioning, you need to strengthen your fearless muscle. The more you take on things that scare or unnerve you, the easier it gets to do this. I've actually practiced using this muscle to a point where I now welcome the things that frighten me. I know my mistakes will always lead to learned gifts. I'd rather show up on the field to play and be in my life, than miss any more precious moments of getting to know and be me in this lifetime.

As we all know, life has a limited timeframe and an expiration date. While I'm aiming to get to 96, in truth, none of us really knows our own expiration date. For me, each day has to be played with the intention of giving it my all and doing my best. While I'm still in physical form, I want to do all I can to leave this planet a lot more loving, kind, and full of people like you who are able to feel and emanate self-love and peace. Please keep building and developing your courage muscle. It is worth every ounce of your effort!

Creating a beginner's mind

Ever heard of the concept of "shoshin?" My wise and loving husband, Heath, first introduced this concept to me when I was discussing a situation where I felt a little self-entitled. I asked twice what he meant, and again in my own ego-mind, I was thinking, "How could he know a self-help word that I didn't know after all the years of personal development work?" Once I got over myself and became grateful for his calm presence, I inquired more about shoshin.

Shoshin means beginner's mind in Zen Buddhism. I've studied a bit of this through yoga and Buddhist teachings. To come to the table with a beginner's mind means that I have no preconceptions, judgments, or stories to hang my hat on. Only then can I be truly open, like a sponge, ready to soak new learning and experiences with curiosity. There's no room with shoshin to get stuck in limited thoughts, crappy old stories, or lingering self-deprecating affirmations. The challenge is to remind us as often as possible to be in a state of reception and of nothingness. When you choose to be this, you can be like a child who is curious, eager, and inquisitive. You are enthusiastic, willing to jump in, get dirty, fall down, and get right back up. When you choose a beginner's mind, you will embark upon an amazing adventure full of wonderment, surprises, lessons and a journey you'd never want to miss.

ACTIVITY:
When thoughts such as, "I'm not good enough" or "I am not experienced enough" get in the way, I say these five thoughts instead:

- I am learning every day.
- I love learning something new about myself.
- This new experience is going to serve in my self-development.
- Life is a classroom and I'm always learning.
- Another growth opportunity!

Your turn:

When thoughts like _____
_____ **get in my way, I will instead train my mind to say these five new thoughts**
(or feel free to adopt mine):

1.

2.

3.

4.

5.

"What I've learned is that giving my 100%
doesn't look the same each day; however, I am always willing
to be authentic and remain open to new ideas."

~Julie Reisler

Chapter 4 Tap-into-You Journal Space

Journal about what you will try that you were too fearful to previously attempt. Note how your mindset changed around fear. How are you using a beginner's mind?

journal

TAP INTO YOU

space

"My super power is . . ."

"The journey
of a thousand miles
begins with a single
step."

~Lao Tzu

Bless the Baby Steps

A s a recovering compulsive perfectionist, doing anything in baby steps used to seem virtually impossible. The miracle here—and I don't take the word lightly—is that today I not only welcome the baby steps, I have learned to bless them. If I can change my way of navigating through life by honoring my small micro-movements, then I know this is possible for you, too. What does that look like in our fast-paced, high-tech, and web-based world that focuses on before and after shots, drama, and big changes? It means redefining life on your terms.

First of all, we never really see all the work that went into someone going from a couch potato to a bikini body. I'm pretty sure there are photo editors and PR firms we can thank for those quick results always being thrust at us as reality. I'm discovering that all wisdom and learning can be seen organically from what Mother Nature does naturally. Look at how a tree releases its leaves in autumn, focuses energy inward in winter, sprouts buds in the spring, and grows new leaves in the summer. That growth doesn't happen overnight.

Practice those baby steps

As human beings, we naturally grow and evolve behaviors over time. There are numerous studies around how our brains work that support the understanding that new thought patterns and habits take time, practice, and repetition. When we practice new thoughts or behaviors, our brain neurons literally start hanging out together and create whole new pathways that lead to the changes we desire. If you start to embrace all movements forward, even when it appears like you're going backwards, you'll develop your muscles of self-compassion and self-encouragement, which reinforce your desire to practice your new behavior more.

As someone who is more oriented towards impatience and wanting the big win now, I have been in intensive baby-step boot camp. I am training myself to honor and celebrate any small changes, while keeping my heart and eyes focused on my larger vision. You are cordially invited to join me in the baby-step boot camp. I'm pretty sure you will dig the results. Let's try an exercise to get a sense of how you might apply this to your life experience.

Grab your favorite pen, journal, or laptop and let's see what opens up here!

1. Look at a big win in your life and write it down. If you're feeling adventurous, write two or three. For example, leaving my stable and cushy job to start my own biz.

2. When you analyze how this big change or goal was met, can you break down the time frame? For me, the first thing I did when I thought of leaving my job was to imagine how I'd coach clients...then I thought about who might be interested in coaching...and then I started to think of what kinds of clients I'd want to coach...until I chose a name, registered for a website and began from the bottom up creating my business. List the steps YOU took here.

When you are planting anything, you get the soil ready, plant your seeds, and then water and nurture it a little most days. You don't yank up the seeds to see if they are growing. That would inhibit the growth process. Over the course of time, with more care, love, and action, your seeds sprout and then bloom to become a beautiful array of flowers. These changes happen—sometimes more slowly than imagined. We don't always know what the seed-to-flower timeline is, yet we do know that most delicious aspects of life happen one baby step at a time.

Are you starting to see how crucial these blessed baby steps are? Sometimes that looks like getting to the gym three days in a row and then taking three days off to binge-watch your favorite shows. If you stay in the cycle of judging yourself, you'll probably be on the couch for another week, month, or even a year. Instead, find a glimmer of self-compassion and truly honor yourself for going three days in a row. Embrace how you felt after that victory. Acknowledge that it can be very challenging to make new habits and stay committed to being your healthiest, most vital self. Be grateful that you started a new pattern of going to the gym and affirm that you are growing stronger every day.

Awareness point: The ego's job is to keep you safe. So the ego sees any change as scary and risky.

Self-sabotage and negative thinking are typical during transitions as your mind adjusts. You have to override ego-mind tendencies as you aim for personal growth. The baby steps help to make this manageable. One of my favorite thought leaders of all time, Oprah Winfrey, says this beautifully: "The key to realizing a dream is to focus not on success but significance—and then even the small steps and little victories along your path will take on greater meaning."

Affirming your new thoughts and behavior can feel weird, even disingenuous, at first. This is a natural part of reprogramming your thoughts to better serve you. Then new action is imperative for a shift to happen. We can't get new results if we stay stuck in the same old habits and behaviors. Once you commit to getting unstuck or to create a transformation, just know that small steps will pay off big time. Most world-class and inspirational leaders will tell you that it is the small incremental habits and daily actions that lead to greatness and big wins. Arianna Huffington, author and co-founder of the Huffington Post, says it brilliantly: "But you have to do what you dream of doing even while you're afraid."

I encourage you to be kind, gentle, and caring with yourself as you take new steps. You would never yell at a ten-month old baby for taking a step, falling, crawling, and trying again. You would cheer him on. After much practice, tears, falling down, and parents championing more steps forward, babies eventually learn how to walk. This is a great lesson for us adults.

Here are more questions to ask yourself:

Where can you see an area in your life that would benefit from baby steps?

What could those baby steps be?

How might you celebrate your baby steps?

Whom can you share your baby steps with? This will help you learn to accept, support, and develop the practice of sharing yourself authentically. You may not know it, but you are also offering them a gift by modeling how to create change.

"Keep the mantra alive—baby steps are your golden ticket to lasting change." ~Julie Reisler

Chapter 5 Tap-into-You Journal Space

Journal about the most important baby steps you took this week and where you envision them leading. Review what area in your life would most benefit from baby steps. Consider what those baby steps might be.

journal

TAP INTO YOU

space

"I will celebrate my baby steps by . . ."

"I AM,
two of the most powerful words,
for what you put after them
shapes your reality."

~ Author Unknown

Word Creates Your World

I learned the phrase "word creates your world," from a super smart and highly-trained business leader, Neil Roseman. I met Neil when I was coaching with him in a personal development leadership program. He used these words often to explain his entire philosophy on life. The first time I heard him say this, a lightbulb went off in my head. I had intuited these words, but I had never heard this idea spoken so succinctly. In essence, all of our words are generative. They evoke, develop, and bring forth our reality. We always have the power to choose our words and our reality. I like to think about it like our words (and thoughts) have wings.

To quote Melissa Wadsworth, author of *Collective Manifestation: Heart-Centered Blueprints for Creating Intentional Community*, "The key is that words evoke emotions, sparking both intentional and unintentional outcomes. Words also hold particular vibrations, which are essentially energetic building blocks. When you have awareness around the words you choose, you more powerfully align to what you intend to create."

Think about a moment in your life where you remember saying something hateful, mean, or out of character due to frustration or ignorance. **Can you recall the outcome and the feelings after that incident?**

For example: I remember my devastating 7th grade horror moment when I decided to call my classmate, Jackie DeSanto, a slut. Not only did I not know what that meant, but I was confronted two days later by Jackie and her tight group of friends. They threatened to beat me up if she ever heard me speak about her again. Talk about a word creating an "in your face" reality! I created that whole little drama which came close to resulting in a broken nose. My ignorant words created a frightening world.

Your turn:

Be a word detective

We are 100% responsible for all of our relationships and how they occur. I'm not saying that an abused person deserves an abusive partner. I would be curious to look and see where he or she agreed to be part of that kind of relationship in order to learn and grow. These kinds of victim-perpetrator relationships can be an indicator that a person has limiting thoughts about his or her own self-worth. I hold no judgments about this. We have all struggled with playing the victim or perpetrator in one form or another at various moments of our lives.

Let's do some more digging here. There are some key points that I believe will make all the difference in how you choose to speak and live. One of the quickest ways to assess how others feel about themselves is to listen to the words they say about themselves to others."

For example, I was with a close friend over lunch and I heard her say, "I'll have to sacrifice eating flour and sugar so I can be healthier and lose excess weight." What word jumps out here? Sacrifice. When we think of sacrifice, we think of giving something up, putting in hard work, or maybe even enduring frustration and discontent. I asked her if she'd be open to reframing and rephrasing her sentence just by substituting a few words. Perhaps she could say, "I am open to taking out flour and sugar in order to be in integrity with my body." With that new word choice to support her purpose, she felt motivated, empowered, redirected, excited, and purposeful. That's my idea of a meaningful transformation!

BEFORE:

*"I'll have to sacrifice eating flour and sugar
so I can be healthier and lose excess weight."*

AFTER:

*"I am open to taking out flour and sugar
in order to be in integrity with my body."*

I, too, have struggled with this. I spent years using less-than-supportive words. I've learned from experience that my word choices really do make THE difference. Rather than feeling restricted, my friend felt ready to take on her health. What's really cool about playing and practicing with words is that you'll start to hear your own language and notice when your words do and don't match the outcomes you want. Try it. It's fun to think of yourself as a word detective.

WORD INQUIRY:

1.   What low-energy or disempowering word or phrase do you use too often?

2.   What is a favorite high-energy or empowering word or phrase?

Word creates world in action

The statement "word creates your world" made all the difference in my life when I chose to end my marriage. I knew in my heart it was the best choice for me, and ultimately, for my former husband and children as well. I received some powerful coaching at the time around making this decision. Phill Thomas, one of my mentors and a skilled business leader, said bluntly, "If you knew your life would be wonderful either way—whether you stayed married or not—what would you choose?" I knew in that moment that my answer was to sadly move on. What followed was another life-changing string of words. He said, "Great, Julie. Go do that and make it happen with love, kindness, and generosity."

From that moment on, I proactively chose to end my marriage by focusing on love, kindness, and generosity. For anyone who has ever gone through a divorce, it's rare to have an amicable split. I also credit my former husband for being kind, gracious, and generous with the ease of our transition. Actually, I don't call him my ex-husband; I call him my Co-Parenting Partner or my CPP.

I embarked on one of my saddest, most challenging and grueling life events with the powerful choice to use words that would support the outcome I wanted. If I truly wanted to forge an amicable and workable partnership, there was no room for being mean-spirited or unkind. My experience was shaped by focusing on the positive words that carried me through our split.

No matter what life situation you have created or are encountering, you always have the choice to choose your words and language to support your best self. I'm not saying it will always be easy, especially when you feel victimized or entitled to something. I can tell you that committing to being loving, kind, and benevolent—no matter what—made all the difference and actually left me feeling more empowered to take on my whole new life in the same way. Let's try an activity to start playing with this concept.

Choosing your mindset

Your body is a natural wealth of information, so we're going to play with tuning and tapping into that innate intelligence. I want you to notice how your body feels with each example and where you feel more or less energized.

SCENARIO 1

You are feeling lethargic and frustrated that you have not been using your gym membership and can't fit into your college clothes.

Which phrase would you be more likely to say to yourself?

A.   *I am a failure at following through and I won't ever fit into my hip college pants again.*

B.   *I have no time to do anything for myself, so I am going to give away all of my pre-weight gain clothes.*

C.   *I have yet to follow through on going to the gym. I'm committed to being healthy and will look at my calendar to schedule self-care dates at the gym.*

Which of the three is going to help you feel empowered to act and make a shift? For my defeatist sistas (and bros) out there, it's not choice A or B. Most of us are motivated by positive encouragement.

Here's another scenario to try on for size.

SCENARIO 2

You work very hard at your job but have a difficult time getting raises or are passed over for promotions.

What do you tell yourself?

A.   *It's not fair. I'm not seen as the leader I know I am. I can't stand the way this office works! My CEO, Rachel, definitely likes my colleagues better. I'm going to start my job search since I'm not good enough for her.*

B.   *I'm bummed I've not been asked to take on more cool projects. I wonder if there's something I've been doing or not doing to cause my manager to not see my value? I know she wants the best for our firm, and I want to make a difference and contribute. I am going to see if I can chat with her to inquire how I can improve.*

Awareness of one's true abilities and reflection on possible steps produces a more positive outlook. You can practice holding a positive outlook by reframing situations so that you are back in charge of your choices as to next actions and steps. Life really works this way. We go through each situation constantly making meaning of all that's happening around us. As you practice using new words, I'd strongly encourage you to practice listening to the words you say to yourself and others. The clues are all there. The more you get in tune with your body and how you perceive your life situations, the more you'll be able to feel how certain words support affirmative steps and outcomes. Learning to tune into your body is a fabulous, free tool that is always available to you.

Let's put this in real time with your everyday life. **Write down an area where you feel stuck or frustrated.**

What did you or do you tell yourself about this situation?

Now list new ways to view this same situation. Try to create at least two positive points of view.

One new way to view this situation is:

A second perspective on this situation is:

A third perspective on this situation is:

A fourth perspective on this situation is:

The brand-new view I am open and eager to take on is:

Look at your first response and check in to see how that made you feel.
· Are you more or less energized?
· Are you inspired to take action?
· Do you want to crawl into the fetal position?

Now, check your responses for the next four actions. Can you see a correlation between the words you use and the way you interpreted the situation?

We often have to create new ways to look for a new perspective. Consider that one of the key things that keeps us stuck or conversely, helps us to feel courageous, empowered, and willing to change, is the words we use.

I have changed my way of talking about "tough life situations" and instead call them "growth opportunities." Just changing my language leads to a paradigm shift every time I encounter something that could feel challenging. You, too, can welcome growth and learning opportunities that help you to develop more wisdom, life smarts, experience, strength, and grit.

"When you change the way you look at things, the things you look at change."
~ Esther Hicks, Ask and It Is Given: Learning to Manifest Your Desires

Practice in the present

A few years ago I was stuck on the road in an extensive and pretty frightening snowstorm with about 2% visibility. I was anxious, annoyed, scared to drive, and I almost pulled over. After taking a few deep breaths, saying a few prayers, and calling my sweetheart to vent, I reminded myself that this was an awesome opportunity to both appreciate the glittery snow and learn how to drive successfully in any terrain and weather. I felt my body relax and let go. I put on some meditative music and drove about three miles per hour with the belief that I was gaining a new skill. Okay, it took me two hours to go five miles, but I came away feeling lit up and grateful to be alive.

A SEVEN-DAY WORD EXERCISE:
Jot down or record the unhelpful/non-supportive words you use with others as well as what you tell yourself. I'd recommend getting a small journal or finding a good recording app so you don't forget if you don't have this book handy when it happens.

For example, write down when you say something like, "I'm an idiot for forgetting my keys." Next, write down how that made you feel, such as being annoyed, jealous, less-than, excited, eager. Lastly, write down a new positive way to talk to yourself. Try it out now.

Write something negative you said to yourself recently:

How does that make you feel?

What is positive phrase you could say instead?

How does that make you feel?

Keep at it. My hunch is that you will start to notice a pattern in your speech. The intention is to increase your awareness of what you are actually saying to yourself and to others about yourself. Interrupting negative self-talk helps you take charge of how you feel about yourself and what you are capable of.

Don't forget that our bodies are always listening. I'll never forget the moment I learned that our gut has more sensory neurons than our brain. The gut is many times referred to as the second brain. I would invite you to consider that our bodies and minds are way more intertwined than we can fathom. Just knowing scientifically that our gut is linked to our brain hopefully gives some possibility to see this connection. I mention this to drive home the point again about watching our words. As the author and motivational speaker Mike Dooley says, "Thoughts become things."

The world of AND

I'm now going to introduce you to one of my favorite words of all time. It's a simple, three-letter word that changed my life. That word is simply: AND. I learned from practice that swapping the word BUT with AND could change my world. It's astounding and it's been a game changer for me. I've now become the "But Police." When we use the word BUT we're inherently saying that there's only room for one way to do something. It squashes out possibility.

For example, "I want to run outside and work out today, BUT it's too cold." In that statement, you've already decided there's no room for possibly running. It's like the BUT gives you an out. Now try on, "I want to run outside and work out today, AND it's too cold." You still might choose not to run; however, by using AND, you are creating a possibility to get your BUTT outside running or find an indoor place to run.

Let's try another example, "I need more sleep, BUT there's a lot to do at night after the kids go to sleep," versus "I need a lot more sleep AND there's a lot to do at night after the kids go to bed." See the difference, my friends? In the first example, it seems impossible to get more sleep. Door closed, not happening, too much to do. You just wrote off any chance of seeing where you can tweak your schedule. In the second sentence, the word AND allows for the potential to get more sleep and do chores after the kids go to sleep.

Can you imagine how often we limit ourselves with our words? Start taking note of when you say BUT and replace it with AND to see how you feel afterwards. You're also going to start noticing where and when others do the same. My "But Police" siren goes off frequently with myself. Are you ready to take on the world of AND? I promise you will notice yourself taking amazing new actions and becoming more of the person you want to be.

Here's a fun list of words and phrases to use in the place of ones that don't serve your highest good. I challenge you to become your own word detective. When these less-than-kind words pop up, know you're headed to limited-thinking land. The quickest way to adjust your course is to change your words and, as a result, your thoughts. Here are some new affirming words and phrases to try on instead: Keep the list going; what other words can you add here? Your turn.

Instead of:	Say this:
Failure	Learning opportunity
But	And
Crisis	Opportunity for growth
Perfection	Focused to do my best
I'm unable	I don't know how yet
I'm trapped	Another way has yet to be revealed
I never have	I have yet to do this
I never will	All is possible
I can't picture it	I'm open and willing to picture it
I am always the one who...	I'm willing to let go of thoughts of being the martyr that don't serve me or others
I'm an idiot	I am constantly learning from all situations
Can't	Not yet
Won't	Perhaps someday
Busy	Full
Why me?	What can I learn here?
This happened again to me	What do I need to change to alter this outcome?
I don't have the money	I'm an abundant human being in many ways

"In essence, all of our words evoke, develop, and bring forth our reality. We always have the power to choose our words and our reality." ~Julie Reisler

Chapter 6 Tap-into-You Journal Space

Write about the negative things you say aloud or tell yourself silently. For example, write down when you say something like, "I'm an idiot for forgetting my keys." Next, write down how that made you feel, such as being annoyed, jealous, less-than, excited, or eager. The intention is to increase your awareness of what you are actually saying to yourself, to others about yourself, and how those words make you feel. Then replace those words and statements with positive alternatives.

journal

TAP INTO YOU

space

"When I look at the tough situations in my life, I realize that…"

"The best way to
predict the future
is to create it."

~ Peter Drucker

Brand Spankin' New Stories

This is one of my favorite topics, because when I truly understood how my stories worked in my life, I had a huge mind shift. It was like I saw the whole world through dingy yellow glasses, and then all of a sudden my lenses became crystal clear. After years of self-study, personal development and transformational programs, and more than $10,000 in therapy, I can say with certainty that our stories create our lives. Countless friends, peers, coaching clients, and mentors have also discovered this powerful truth.

A better story

As human beings, we are constantly trying to find meaning by making up stories about the world around us. Throw in the propensity for the human brain to focus on negatively-slanted stories, and we're left with a whole slew of stories that don't serve our highest good. Here's the other interesting part to understand—our life events are concrete, yet how we interpret those events is where things can get super funky.

Given that there are infinite ways to make meaning of our life occurrences, every person will have a different slant on their interpretation. What's even more mind blowing here is that we not only act as if our version of our story is the only one, but we also accept it as the truth. Here's the rub—phenomena (observable events like who, what, when, how, where) and story (the meaning you assign to the experience) aren't the same.

For example, Josie failed her real estate exam. The phenomenon is that she studied for, took, and failed the exam. Josie's story around those events is that she is a failure and will never be able to help clients buy their dream home. It's easy to see how we can get very stuck in our particular stories and limit our ability for infinite possibilities.

Here's another example of perspective. I'm looking to change jobs or get back in the career force. I'm on a mission to interview with my top three companies. I get dressed, put on tights without a run, and coordinate my jewelry only to snag my tights on my decorative ring (damn that ring)! I get in my car with my résumé, ready to go, and somehow get lost. I finally find the correct turn and have trouble finding parking. I'm starting to feel that this interview is not going to work out well (story one). In fact, I'm now pretty sure that my chances of getting this job are slim to none (more dramatic story). The cards feel stacked against me (more of same old story).

I'm going to pause here to consider two possible outcomes. If I continue running with my storyline of "Everything is going wrong and I'm doomed," guess what my interview experience will be? It's guaranteed that when I go in with the belief that I'm not good enough, I'll be frustrated, negative, and certainly convince my potential new employers that I shouldn't land the job. However, if I can see that I'm starting to weave a pretty compelling "Woe is me" story, I can stop in my tracks, affirm that I have a lot to offer, perhaps breathe deeply, and assume they are going to adore imperfect me.

Another thing that can shift you into positive energy is the "victory pose." Whether you're lying down on your bed with arms and legs outstretched, or you're standing in the shape of an X, this move is physiologically proven to boost your mood. No joke. I highly recommend you try it (and it's free). To get the maximum benefits, do this pose for 2 minutes. If you're short on time, 30 seconds will do.

I know from personal experience that what I tell myself will determine how my message is delivered, how I'm interacting with others, and how my life turns out. If you want to see what thoughts and stories you're telling yourself, look at how life is showing up today.

Now imagine a past story. Let's say you felt uncomfortable in your skin as a kid. You were constantly reminded to eat less by your mom and never got asked out by any of the boys you liked. Can you see a story line forming here? You might start believing that your body is not to be cherished and loved. You might think that you need to lose weight in order to find romance and happiness. I know this story well because this was me. I believed I was not good enough, my body was not to be loved, and that I would be lucky if any guy liked me. Talk about a disempowering context. If not dismantled, such a story could become part of your inner fabric of beliefs and you could weave more thoughts of body loathing and insecurity into your life tapestry. I continued to live out this exact story for a long time until I realized I was accepting a very limited approach and understanding of my early life encounters.

A lot of our feeling stuck, trapped, insecure, angry, resentful, and unsafe is based on how we interpret what happened. If we learn from a parent (or society) to always look for the negative side, we will most likely repeat this approach. My mom, one of the most positive, loving, and caring people on the planet, did hand me a gift by helping me look at life situations through rose-colored glasses. However, I wasn't able to do it most of the time until I learned the trick. The secret here is not to change others—the real lesson is to change your story.

Once you realize you have total control over how to interpret life situations, it's just a matter of time before you are able to be aware and practice finding creative new ways to see your life. The biggest gift you can give yourself is being in the driver's seat. You have to see yourself as empowered and in charge of the way you view and understand your life. For me, this perspective is fun to play around with.

Just as importantly, I also had to get over wanting to get even, be right, and be willing to let go of outdated beliefs. Here's the other profound thing I realized—why not start making up stories that serve me and my life? Why not choose new perspectives and stories that will leave you feeling grateful and at ease?

Connecting the DOTS

Before digging in to find your limiting stories, I'd like you to consider that we all have a Default Operating and Tracking System or DOTS for short. This is how we show up, track past events, carry them into the future, and metaphorically connect the dots. In order to connect these dots, we have to first understand that our current beliefs and stories—especially if not checked out, reviewed, reappraised, and consciously questioned—are based on our upbringing. Whether they come from our parents, friends, peers, societal programming, education system, first breakup, first fight, first love, or any of the varied experiences encountered over one's life journey, I absolutely believe that we can change our DOTS at any time.

I grew up in a house where food was used to show love. Can I get an "Amen"? My dad, bless his food-loving heart, would bring home crazy amounts of fresh breads, pies, and treats for no reason. One of my first memories is Dad stopping for two chocolate-covered chocolate donuts with chocolate sprinkles on the way to dropping me at nursery school. I knew my dad loved me to pieces, and a big way that was shown was through food.

From that experience, I created a story that in order to show love, I should buy and bake treats. More importantly, I integrated the belief that food was the best way to cope with all emotions. If I was sad, angry, envious, tired, happy, bored, bummed, elated, or neutral, food was my go-to answer. To me food equaled love and self-love. I don't blame my dad one bit, because somewhere I chose to adopt that meaning. It wasn't until I started to feel completely out of control with my eating that I questioned this story. I realized that not only did I have a problem with food, but also with my story around what constitutes self-love and true nourishment.

I love how our biggest challenge can become our greatest strength. It took some time for me to understand the truth about my deep-rooted connection to food. And I still deal with moments of buying into my old story. However, my new DOTS today is all about nourishing my mind, body, and soul with foods, thoughts, practices, and movements that are loving and of service to my higher purpose. No way could I write this book, take the leap of faith to leave my cushy nine-to-five job, or run my own business, if I were merely existing under my old, limiting DOTS.

It's now time for YOU to connect your DOTS.

I want to first acknowledge you for being brave enough to look at yourself and your life to see what's there. Shedding light on your stories allows the healing power of awareness and understanding to work on releasing limiting thoughts.

"Our head and thoughts can be likened to a dangerous neighborhood. We should never go there alone." I heard this at a 12-step meeting and never forgot it. We bring limiting beliefs into the light by choosing to take a look at what's hiding in the dark corners of our unconscious minds. You can do this on your own, through a workbook like this, through a support group, or along with accountability partners to share the process with. Hint: This is a great time to review your teamsters.

As a human being, you all have acquired and made up stories that don't serve your true greatness. Know that confronting the truth of your stories can feel really uncomfortable. It's not uncommon to experience pain, grief, and frustration when you let go of old beliefs in order to rewire your incredible brain for new thought patterns and stories. Just tell yourself that it's totally cool to let go of old beliefs, try a new mode of living, and be open to new truths and possibilities. You can always go back to life as usual if you want. You are always the driver. Don't forget—breakdowns and breakups lead to breakthroughs. Like a rainbow, you may have to first experience the storm before you fully show up. It takes time and courage to try something new. You've totally got this. I know because you're reading and using this workbook.

DOTS assessment

In order to get a sense of some of your DOTS, let's look at how you view these specific areas of your life. Here are some questions to ask yourself:

What is my core belief about life? (Such as, "It all works out in the end," "Life is a crazy ride and I'm not the driver," "The world is an impersonal place," "There is more to life than meets the eye.")

How did this core belief develop? (Did I adopt it from my family, read it somewhere, realize it from my experiences?)

Do you have any explicit memories around these five areas that shaped your world view? When did they happen, who was involved, and what idea or belief emerged from the experience?

1.   Family *(For example, "My mom screamed at me often as I was growing up, and I found myself screaming to get my own child's attention. It felt like a natural reflex. It wasn't until a neighbor told me she could hear me screaming and that it made her sad to hear, that I reflected on this.")*

2.   Career

3.   Religion and Spirituality

4.   Health and Well-being

5.   Relationships

Trying on a new view

It's okay to have something come up that you realize doesn't truly represent how you want to think or how you want to be in the world. This is a great place to be. We can't change without awareness, so we need to see what's going on before we can make a shift.

This showed up for me around sports. I was a decent dancer and swimmer, but I was not a great soccer player. My personal strengths didn't matter since I believed that soccer was the only sport that mattered because it was such a huge deal in my hometown of Newton, MA. My dad coached me for 10 years, always trying to get me to love it more. My best friend Meg was crazy awesome and even got recruited to play Division I soccer at Harvard. When I went to college, I did not even make the intramural team. The truth is, I didn't love playing soccer because I was scared shitless of getting hurt or hurting someone else. Probably not the greatest mentality when playing sports.

So I assumed I was not an athlete. I even gave up all sports for four years. Then one day I was listening to Dave Matthews in my dorm room and I remembered that I loved to dance! That prompted me to enroll in two dance classes my senior year at University of Rochester. I realized that I had been caught up in a not-good-enough story about myself. This feeling of lack was amplified by a specific physical fitness story my family and community supported that "soccer was king." This had prevented me from finding enjoyment and fulfillment through other forms of movement and exercise. No more. Today I'm a certified barre instructor, fitness instructor, and personal trainer.

This is just one small example about what happens when you start seeing how your stories about who you are affect your relationships, career, vision for yourself, and your life as a whole. This is crazy powerful and sacred work. You are looking below the surface at what you believe to be true to perceive where you might be hanging on to someone else's belief. What's even more amazing and freeing is when you realize that you are carrying around someone else's story, and you choose to let it go. It's like dropping a 30-lb. bag of rocks. Get ready to feel lighter, calmer, and more peaceful. Who doesn't want that?

Reimagining your stories

While it may be hard to imagine, I promise it's possible to rewrite your storyline and free yourself from others' perspectives, past events, or upsetting encounters. It's also an opportunity to start dreaming, think expansively, and envision your most extraordinary new story.

Here's one of the coolest things I've noticed as I've taken responsibility as the empowered author of my stories and life. Given my belief that we can't change others, only ourselves, I have noticed a kick-butt byproduct of changing me. The people in my world and circles start to show up differently for me.

For example, my friend Mona could question my choice to pose nude for an artist's painting and even comment that I'm crazy. This might have triggered feelings before of being judged. With my new story of everyone mirroring his or her own stuff, this allows me to see that Mona's stories don't allow her to pose nude. For me, I don't have any stories that cause me to judge this action. I might just do it for free in the name of art. (By the way, I made up this scenario. I've yet to pose nude, just in case you were wondering!)

It has taken years of self-work, lots of body-love affirmations, and recreating the "house I live in" to get to the point of even contemplating such an activity. Rather than feeling upset at people who think differently, I feel compassion, care, and understanding. I now have more ability to hold space for others to be as they are, and as a result, I attract more open-minded and caring humans. Can you think of a time where you changed your perspective on something and thus changed how you were being? If not, watch, observe, and see what happens. The real-deal secret sauce here is that when we shift our beliefs and stories, the world seems to shift around us (*A-ha!* is right).

Give your new story a whirl

Ready to give it a go? Since you now know we are all creating stories, I want you to think about what you'd like your new story to look like. Take time and space here to write it out. Anything goes, and I'm inviting you to feel free to write it fairytale-style or however you'd like to see your story play out. Feel free to do more creating of your story in the journal prompts and coloring pages to follow. Remember, this is your life, your next chapter, and your story that you get to create.

"The secret here is not changing others—
the real lesson is to change your story." ~Julie Reisler

"The real-deal special sauce here is when we choose to shift our beliefs
and stories, the world seems to shift around us." ~Julie Reisler

Chapter 7 Tap-into-You Journal Space

This week use your journal space to affirm what you are realizing and learning about yourself. Note what you have learned about your current DOTS [Default Operating and Tracking System] and how you would like to change this mental system so you are more conscious.

journal
TAP INTO YOU
space

"Once upon a time, I (fill in your name) was the greatest..."

My favorite affirmation
when I feel stuck or out-of-sorts
is, "Whatever I need is already here,
and it is all for my highest good."
Jot this down and post it
conspicuously throughout your home,
on the dashboard of your car, at
your office, on your microwave oven,
and even in front of your toilets!

~ Wayne Dyer

Affirming YOU!

Affirmations are a great way to overwrite the human tendencies to believe the negative things our minds tell us and to compare ourselves to others. Affirmations are like a great makeover. I always love a great makeover, don't you? So let's do a makeover with our words. What I've found to truly work is to string supportive words together into an affirmation. Remember, as human beings we're going to make stories anyway, so let's start practicing optimistic language and affirmations to encourage our awesome new stories. Ready to see miracles take shape in your life?

My favorite self-help guru, Louise Hay, wrote books on the power of hearing and saying affirmations. For all you doubters—maybe even haters—out there, affirmations are worth a try. Even just for the fact that they are free of charge.

Affirmations that work for me might not be your cup of affirmation tea. You can change these suggested affirmations to fit your taste and personality. All of us have different needs, dreams, visions, and ultimately unique stories we wish to carry out. So, are you now ready for the affirmation game? Let's jump in!

Here is a list of some of my absolute favorite affirmations:

Affirmation playlist:

·   I am letting go of anything that doesn't serve me.

·   I am willing and open to releasing all negative thoughts and stories.

·   I am ready now to be fully me.

·   It is safe to be fully me and present.

·   I affirm that I am a divine being full of love and compassion.

·   I am ready to accept all the beauty in my life.

·   I am grateful for the multitude of blessings in my life.

·   I cultivate an attitude of gratitude in all areas of my life.

·   I am safe and taken care of in all areas of my life.

·   I am willing to release any excess physical or energetic weight, insecurities, or habit patterns that do not serve my highest good.

·   I know that my body is releasing anything it doesn't need to be balanced, efficient, and well.

- I am willing to move towards my optimal health, well-being, and love my body more.
- I honor, cherish, and love the house I live in fully, and I marvel at the miracles of how it works effortlessly.
- I choose to nourish my mind with loving and supportive thoughts.
- I choose awesome words to create new stories which are giving me my best life.
- All is well, and I have everything I need to thrive and be abundant.
- I am the author of my own life and get to write my story.
- I am abundant in all areas of my life.
- I choose my life to be full of abundance and joy.
- I choose to be abundant in words, thoughts, actions, and deeds with others.
- I attract all forms of abundance in my life now.
- With willingness and openness, all things are possible for me to accomplish.
- I am a divine being intricately connected to my human brothers and sisters.
- I choose to fully shine my light, knowing that doing so allows others to do the same.
- I am enveloped in divine love and blessed beyond belief.
- Other people's opinions and judgments of me are none of my beeswax.
- I release anyone who is playing a negative role for me.
- I choose my attitude and outlook on life.
- I am perfect as I am today: whole, complete, and wise.
- Anything I need to know will come to me at exactly the right time.
- My birthright is joy, love, and blessings.
- I choose to see everything today as a miracle.

Fine-tune your affirmations!

These are a starting point for you. Write down the top five affirmations that resonate most strongly with you. Tweak and edit as you see fit.

You are the only one who can make a change for yourself. Whenever you hear or catch yourself saying something negative, replace it with something positive. Start developing your new habit pattern around affirming what you do want, not what you don't want. You can train your incredible brain at any time to think in new ways. Remember, our brains are malleable, so we are always able to change it in a positive direction. The key is that change starts with you. Keep a running list of the affirmations that resonate with you. I am confident that you'll find wittier and more personalized ways to affirm all the good on its way into your life.

Affirmation tips

When creating affirmations, start with the following phrases:

I am	I affirm	I create
I am willing	I love	I attract
I release	It is safe to	I appreciate
I am open to	I am grateful for	I am expanding
I allow	I am attracting	
I am ready now	I choose to	

Your turn. Start your own list of your favorite affirmations using the sentence starters above.

Daily Magical Practices #2: Affirmation through celebration

Each day you have reason to celebrate. Start a practice of celebrating YOU. Celebrate being alive, getting to know and love yourself, extending that love to others, receiving opportunities to learn and grow, and being present for the magic of life.

Growth is to be celebrated and honored because any change in a healthy direction, no matter how small, is an excellent change. Your thoughts, beliefs, and actions created who you are and who you are becoming. Keep planting your favorite and most fruitful seeds. Don't forget to collect the bouquet of flowers you have grown. Life is about joy and enjoyment. The good news is that there is only more flourishing to come. You are on the journey of growing your best life!

Time to celebrate, my friends! Please don't overlook this important daily practice; rejoice by injecting each day with the flavor of celebration and doing something super sweet for yourself. As humans we tend to devalue our existence and our profound effect on others. As you start to celebrate daily, you will recalibrate your celebration mentality. You'll find more to celebrate.

Celebration may be as simple as using a joyous daily affirmation to set the tone of the day, doing something intentionally kind for others, and/or celebrating yourself. For instance:

1. Each morning say to yourself, "I celebrate YOU! I celebrate all that you are. I celebrate living as a reflection of wholeness." You can reword this in any way you like. Pick your moment: as you get out of bed, brush your teeth, commute to work, have lunch, make dinner, or in your journal in the evening.

2. Schedule a personal celebration! This doesn't have to cost money. Taking a hot bath with sea salts and lighting a candle with Enya in the background is one of my favorite celebrations. What constitutes a celebration to you?

3. Celebrate your connectedness. Set the intention to do something kind for someone else each day or to recognize when you do something kind naturally. By putting more attention on your positive actions, you will appreciate and affirm how connected you are to others and how special these connections are—even the briefest encounters.

4. Start a celebration vision board showing gratitude for what is currently good in life or some other specific theme that ties in with celebration of life. Add something to this board daily. Share it with a loved one or make it a daily practice to look at it each morning. When will you commit to beginning this practice?

5. Celebrate play by making time for kid-like fun activities like ice skating, roller skating, miniature golf, water parks, or paint ball: whatever it is that allows you to feel child-like in the moment having crazy fun. Do it and don't wait. And better yet, schedule a few dates!

"What would get your butt up at 3 A.M.?
Therein, my friends, lies a great clue
about how to get unstuck and get moving."
~Julie Reisler

Chapter 8 Tap-into-You Journal Space

Use this space to note what you have learned about affirmations. How might you make affirmations more fun?

journal

TAP INTO YOU

space

"*I know I am living on purpose when I am . . .*"

"Love yourself first,
and everything else
falls in line. You really have
to love yourself to get
anything done in this world."

~Lucille Ball

The Power of Self-Care and Nourishment

Do you truly care for YOU? Self-care is one of the most important factors of moving from self-loathing and insecurity to self-worth and confidence. There is an inherent power available to you when you make an effort to steadily love your whole self. Some might see self-care as selfish, but it's actually the opposite. You are either replenishing your energy or depleting it. Without self-care it's difficult to consistently offer others your support, good will, and optimism. You can't give away what you don't have. Whether you want to be a better friend, partner, leader, parent, or spouse, it all starts with your capacity and ability to love and care for yourself.

It is important to love your whole self. By whole self I mean mind, emotions, body, and spirit. Whether or not you believe in God or a higher power, we are all looking for a connection to the fullness of who we are.

I believe that our connection to others, the Earth, animals, and ourselves is one of our main reasons for inhabiting this planet. I have seen some of my best work and most amazing life connections come right after I invested time and energy in myself. We will now look at several ways to practice self-care.

Making time for self-care

You might find the idea of taking more time out of your busy schedule for self-care to seem impractical, scary, weird, or even difficult. At first, I was filled with guilt and disbelief. How could spending $30 on a manicure to sit and do nothing make a difference for others? My dear friend and mentor, Paula, used to say, "The more you add love to yourself, the more life will love you back." Self-care is self-love in action. It is about aligning to your inherent value. You are saying to yourself, "My well-being matters."

The whole martyr concept is one that can be an easy hook for women: especially busy mothers or anyone with a tendency to rescue others or to put others before self. Somehow we are taught to believe that in order to be a caring, good, and special person, we must forfeit self-care. This is a huge myth. It is not unusual for women and men who feel like all they do is give, to end up feeling drained, overwhelmed, resentful, and void of true connection. To truly make a difference in the world, be it with your children, friends, family, pets, neighbors, community, religious groups, or the planet at large, you must find a way to recharge your battery and refuel. Let's look at nourishment in all forms.

Nourishing yourself

When you hear the word nourishment, what comes to mind? Perhaps you think of food, although just having access to food doesn't mean you're fully nourished or getting important nutrients.

Nourishment can also relate to emotional fulfillment or being satisfied with your life activity. It might relate to how you express your spiritual nature. I'd invite you to unpack this word in a few ways as it relates to your mind, emotions, and body. How does it connect to your overall well-being?

How do you choose to nourish your mind? Do you read self-help books or subscribe to e-newsletters about healthy living? Do you know what depletes your mental nourishment? For me, it is TV programs with any kind of negative drama, reality television, and the news. (No judgment if you adore these shows; I totally get it.) Your mind is like a garden, which needs fertile soil, rich nutrients, water, sunshine, and tender loving care. It makes a difference what you feed your mind.

What about your self-talk? Are you saying mean crap to yourself that you would never in a million years use with your worst enemy? These internal comments make an impact on your mental well-being. In Hal Elrod's book, *Miracle Morning*, he notes that we design our lives, whether we realize it or not, in each moment by what thoughts and actions we choose. He recommends devoting an hour every morning to activities like doing your affirmations, meditating, reading something inspirational, looking at your vision board, journaling, and movement.

How you care and tend to your mind is crucial. Living life on purpose means watching your words and being aware of your DOTS system. It can make a huge difference to feeling nourished. The question to ask yourself is, "Is this serving my mental well-being and nourishing me?" By asking this question, you start to practice making nourishment a priority, focus, and a way of being.

Nourishing pauses

Adding a "pause" button in my life has been a game-changer. For example, when I am exhausted (negative trigger), sometimes I will grab some packaged food (automatic response), eating unconsciously, until I pause and realize that I am darn tired and I simply need a nap to reduce the feeling of edginess. To some people this would seem like common sense. For someone like me with an addictive pattern of using food to cope with my emotions, being able to stop and notice what nourishment I really need feels like a miracle. It's incredible what happens when we take steps forward to love ourselves more!

What pauses could you practice that would help feed your emotional state?

Get into the habit of asking yourself: "What does my body need? Do I need more sleep? More alone time? More time to unplug from technology? More time with friends and family who uplift me? More movement that brings me joy?"

Part of the practice of nourishing yourself is to start knowing how to care for your body. As babies, this is intuitive. Babies eat when they're hungry and stop when they're full. They nap when they're tired and wake up when they are alert. We could learn a lot from babies. Just by asking these new questions, you're priming your brain to think in new terms and in ways that focus on your self care.

So, how the heck are you nourishing yourself? All plants, crops, and living entities need to be nourished, nurtured, and cared for to grow. Last I looked, we're also living entities. Most of us forget this. Many of us nourish ourselves last and give to our families first. Is that you?

Get ready to experience your own nourishment miracles.

What do you need?

We are all born with the capacity to know what we need. Somehow we lose touch with this and we take on bad habits that aren't truly nourishing. Learn to be more mindful. Then pause between your trigger and response. This can look like sitting still for one minute and focusing on breathing. Studies show that when we sit still and breathe, we retrain our brain to pause and increase our ability to react with intention. One of my most favorite quotes is from Viktor Frankl, a holocaust survivor, who said, "Between stimulus and response there is a space. In that space is our power to choose our response. In our response lies our growth and our freedom." What a powerful way to understand life. Oh, and by the way, it's totally free to pause and breathe.

Connection, movement, and self-dates, oh my!

Connection is another area often put to the side in our fast-paced world. There's an abundance of research on the importance of human connection, social bonds, and being able to vent and share with people we trust and love. Not to mention it reminds us we are not alone. It gives the other person a shot at being of service so it's a win-win all around. Connection might also look like finding a spiritual or religious service to attend. Anything goes here. It's all about how you feel most connected to your highest self and the universe.

How about physical movement? This does not mean you have to join a swanky gym. Could you phone a friend and start a new routine of taking beautiful morning walks together? What about a local yoga or Zumba class at your community center or finding a great Pilates class online? Any kind of movement will help keep you feeling more uplifted and nourished, inside and out. It also has loads of benefits for your brain, lungs, heart, and muscle tissue. Regular movement will also improve your posture and your ability to focus, pay attention, and sleep better. Not to mention if you are looking to release any extra weight, movement is crucial.

Self-nourishment is vital to self-love. I suggest making a date with yourself. That's right—go and date you. Take yourself to tea. Get a manicure or a facial. Go on a scenic drive or for a long walk. Take a weekend pottery or painting workshop. You won't have much to give others if you are sucked dry of inspiration. Spending time with yourself will nourish your spirit and give you a new outlook. I'm a huge fan of self-dates. I love knowing I can give myself what I need and find that from within. It's a powerful aspect to creating the strong foundation of self-care and love.

Nourishment in practice

New nourishment practices take patience, persistence, purpose, and pace. Taking baby steps is key. Enjoy being a beginner. This is counterintuitive for many of us, but it will bring about serious life breakthroughs. Without action, all of these suggestions are merely that—nice words you read and miss applying to your life. Consider the following questions:

1. What new mind-body connection action items are you willing to take on? (*For example, I love going to yoga, taking a decadent long shower afterwards, applying spa creams, and buying myself tea.*)

2. Can you add 3–5 minutes of meditation on a daily basis? When? (*This is a free and little change that will be a game changer.*)

3. Where will your self-date be this week? Whom will you tell about it? When is it happening?

4. What new movement activity do you want to try this week? Walking? Yoga? Swimming? Biking? Stretching? Personal training session? Zumba? Pilates?

5. How can you nourish more creativity in your life? *(Be creative here—pun intended.)*

6. What about your relationship to your calendar and time management? Feeling like time is slipping by and you aren't sure where the heck it went? Is there a way to schedule 5 minutes a day to stretch, walk, add some lime to your water, or write a thank you note?

7. Who can you reach out to and connect more with? Don't wait–life is in the now.

Spiritual nourishment

The other imperative to nourishing your mind and body is your connection to yourself and to something greater, whether you call this your higher power, God, Goddess, Mother Earth, Source Energy, Divine Wisdom, the Universe, Great Creator, or Love. Regardless of religion, race, cultural identity, body type, or sexual orientation, we are all made of the same stuff. We are all connected and part of a universal one-ness. It is our purpose and destiny to connect with our true self, with other human beings, and to realize a relationship with all beings in the universe. These connections can be experienced as deep, authentic, true connectedness.

Nourishing our innate need for connection is the real "more" we are seeking.

Grabbing a donut, a glass of whiskey, or high-priced shoes will never fill this wanting of more (although there's nothing wrong with mindfully enjoying earthly pleasures!). The only thing that fills the hole is creating connectedness to ourselves and our divine source. You've got to love you to do this!

A core tenet of this workbook is the idea that creating a life you truly cherish by fully expressing your true self begins with loving yourself. That's why I emphasize again that loving yourself is one of the main secrets to attaining what you want and creating your most cherished life.

Even in the biblical Ten Commandments (even if you're not into religion, I'd consider this part of the Golden Rule) it is written, "Thou shalt love thy neighbor as thyself." It's imperative to see that you can't love your neighbor as yourself if you don't love yourself first. As Mahatma Gandhi so famously pointed out, we become the change we want to see in the world by loving ourselves more and connecting to our highest source.

The second important piece here is to create a reliable connection with your Creator. Feeling yourself as being connected to source energy is part of your DNA. As social beings, we want to connect with others. Yet, by connecting with yourself and divine wisdom first, you will start to realize you are always loved, safe, and cared for. Then your other connections align with your intent to nourish spirit.

Meditative nourishment

Studies show that we can alter our ability to pause, make better choices in the moment, and handle stress through mindfulness and taking breaks.

Sitting and breathing is also known as meditation. Does the word meditation scare the heck out of you? If so, you are so not alone. I used to have a full-blown story I told myself about those who meditate and those who don't. My story made me a member of the latter group. At first, I really struggled with sitting still. My mind wandered all over the place when I tried to meditate. I figured since I wasn't on the top of some beautiful mountain or a Buddhist monk, that I was one of those people who couldn't meditate. I started to write it off as not working for me. Through many weeks of committing to sitting still, regardless of where my mind decided to vacation, I started to feel the profound changes from breathing with stillness. As meditation changed my life, my story about meditation changed.

Meditation is being still in the moment, breathing, and focusing your attention on the here and now. As thoughts come and go, just gently detach and go back to your breath. Being human, your mind is naturally going to wander. This is totally cool and totally normal. Expect it and continue with your intentional breathing anyway. This truly can look like sitting in your PJs on your living room carpet and focusing on your breath. I highly recommend giving this practice a whirl. I started with one minute and now I'm up to twenty minutes. Whether it's one, five, or ten minutes, all of it makes a difference. When I meditate, I can feel a huge change in my stress response, and my ability to handle life situations expands.

I'm a huge Oprah, Tony Robbins, Louise Hay, and Marie Forleo fan, and they all swear by meditative breathing. The more you practice, the more you start to hear what your oh-so-wise body is saying to you. During meditation you not only train your body to communicate with you, you also train your mind to slow down, pause, and have room to get the spiritual nourishment you need.

Learning to listen to your inner voice is a skill that takes practice and patience. I have found this focus to be one of my greatest gifts. When I choose to get still and quiet down, I can hear all sorts of messages and advice from my head and body such as actions to take or not take, needing a nap, impulses to create, or choosing a new idea. I believe we all have and can cultivate this innate inner wisdom. We are complex, evolving beings who deserve all the nourishing ingredients needed to live a bountiful, joyful, and satisfying life.

Fueling nourishment

In addition to creating nourishing thoughts, new stories, the space to feel all of your emotions, movement to keep your body in good working order, and intentional breathing, it's important to look at how you fuel your body (more of this in the next chapter). The concept that food is energy is one that I was not raised with. Nourishing my body was not about tuning in to how I felt or knowing when I felt full. Typically, our meals were more of an intense buffet where you ate as much as you could, as fast as you could, so you could get more. And I mean MORE. I was big into more and as a result, more made me big—I never felt truly full or fulfilled.

There are many ways to connect to your higher self. You may need to override your cultural conditioning for productivity; however, pausing to allow your mind to quiet or engage differently can be one of the most nourishing and important exercises to take on. Your mind needs a break regularly to be at your best and to allow YOU to fully show up. Trust me. I've learned this the hard way after years of pushing myself, only to realize I love life a whole lot more when I take sacred time to slow down.

Can you add a three- to five-minute morning meditation to your day? From my experience, it will pay you huge dividends. Perhaps you would rather devote five to ten minutes to journal writing, recording your dreams, composing a poem, or listening to music.

In addition to meditation, there are many ways to tune into your divine connection:
· prayers from your religious or spiritual tradition
· breath practices
· affirmative positive healing and well-being statements
· morning writing to record dreams, intuitive thoughts, or intentions for the day
· recording your thankfulness in a gratitude journal each evening
· go on a rampage of appreciation (for example, listing anything and everything you are appreciative of in two minutes)

Think of the access to your divine connection as a beautiful buffet (with me, it's always about food). You get to choose what you like most and add it to your plate. Perhaps start with a few items, such as two minutes of breathing each morning, one affirmation about your life, and five written gratitude items before going to bed.

Nourishing your goals

Another awesome side effect to expanding consciousness of your divine connection is that it empowers you to lovingly nourish your desires and to embrace more life abundance. For many people, the practice of feeling connected to a divine source enables them to believe in what they envision and to achieve their goals. By getting clear about your dreams and desires, you are more likely to make it happen. Then, being in gratitude enables you act as if what you desire is already on its way. Esther Hicks, one of my spiritual favorite thought leaders, states that "You are actually pre-paving your future experiences constantly. You are continually projecting your expectations into your future experiences."

For instance, if your goal is to release extra weight, you've got to get clear about what that would "feel" like in order to affirm your belief in your vision of the healthiest version of yourself. As you envision this healthier you, you can be thankful in advance of the outcome, because you firmly trust that your vision is in process. Then it is easier to release the weight you don't need. When self-love drives your dreams and goals, you will attract a loving reality that reflects your best vision for yourself.

When I chose to write this book after a year of first hearing a whisper, then a louder call, to share what I've learned and practiced with others, I envisioned writing with ease and being able to be of service and guide many others who are looking to experience a much more fulfilled life. I saw myself signing inspirational notes in my book. I affirmed that my purpose to coach and inspire others will lead to greater love, joy, and happiness in the world. That inspires me daily and helps me get over my not-good-enough fears. I trust that all who read this will get something, even if only one thing. Remember...

"Self-care is self-love in action." ~Julie Reisler

Chapter 9 Tap-into-You Journal Space

This week, journal about what you learned and practiced around self-love and nourishing yourself. Note if you struggled with any of it. What did you enjoy about this loving process? How does it feel different now that you are connecting more deeply with your body and nourishing it?

journal

TAP INTO YOU

space

"The ways I want to most nourish myself
in mind, body, and spirit, are . . ."

"Take care of your body.
It's the only place you
have to live."

~Jim Rohn

Hungry For More

I am not sure when I lost a sense of listening to my body. I didn't know when to stop eating because I always craved more. I realized around age 14 that I wanted to date boys, but I was outside of the dating circuit. It seemed like everyone else had a boyfriend or at least a boy interested in them by 7th grade except me. Rather than addressing the hurt and pain of feeling rejected, I started to use food to handle these emotions. I wanted more connection and romantic interest. This meant having a boy who wanted to call me (vs. my prank calling boys I liked) and being asked out to a movie, yet because of my limited beliefs about my dating situation, I went to more food.

Getting to the other side of more

Food served its purpose of distracting me from feeling rejected. It was the only way I knew of to get "more" in my life. If you've struggled with using food to cope with life, you know the emptiness of the "more" hole is never filled by food. It is always an insidious illusion. Just like a mirage, I'd think eating a loaf of bread with butter and honey would make me feel better. For a short time, it did. Then I would feel tired, depressed, heavy, bloated, and upset with myself. It only gave me more disconnection, discontent, disease, dis-ease, and depression. The wanting more was really a desire to connect more with myself.

Nourishing my body today with food is about choosing nutrients, vitamins, and foods that are going to best support my body's functioning. This will look different for everyone. I am a big fan of short-term (let me underscore short-term) elimination diets. This is probably the only time you'll hear me use the word "diet" because I'm not a fan of any diet, other than diets from negative self-talk. However, elimination diets allow you to better understand what works best for your body.

For me, giving up sugar was not an easy feat. I felt like an alcoholic getting sober. I was depressed, agitated, had crazy cravings, and poor sleeping habits. I tested out a sugar detox when I was 28 and the results were profound. Three days after my sugar withdrawal symptoms, I started to feel clear-headed, more energetic, calm, centered, more comfortable in my body, and best of all, I wasn't craving sugary stuff. This was my first time understanding the power of sugar and how it wreaked havoc in my life and system. Because I'm quite a stubborn gal, I've dabbled in and out of sugar abstinence for the past decade plus. I've discovered for my body to be most workable, I need to refrain from sugar and white flour products. Sometimes I still miss them, but usually I'm thrilled with the results of not consuming them.

All of our bodies are different, so I'm not advocating this for everyone. However, there is research about the impact sugar has on our brain. It triggers the central reward system in our brain (drugs, alcohol, and sex also affect this part of the brain). My husband can eat four M&M's every evening with no problem, but not me. I'm sure I look at him like he has four heads, because I would never be able to stop at just four. Yet, what used to seem like a prohibition now feels loving, kind, compassionate, and truly nourishing for my body. If you're craving a new relationship to food, you can train yourself to view nourishment in a whole new light.

The varied world of hunger

There is a whole world out there around using our body wisdom with hunger, food, and satisfaction that most of us are missing, myself included. I like to think of my stomach as a gas tank. I never like to get too low in gas and certainly running on fumes is never good for your car. Just like your car, you do best with enough gas in the tank to feel satisfied, satiated, and fueled. It's unnecessary to be full to the brim at all times to run well.

One of the tricks I have learned before meal time is to think about my "gas tank" levels (my stomach and hunger levels). Ideally you want to be somewhat hungry, yet not ravenous. On a scale of 1–10, 1 being starving and 10 being the way you feel after Thanksgiving dinner, you'd want to be at a 3 or 4. I have taught myself to check in and gauge my tank. Try it. It's amazing to notice when you think you are hungry, but after stopping to touch base with your internal cues, you realize you're thirsty or experiencing other types of hunger, such as sight hunger, smell hunger, mouth hunger, or emotional hunger. Let's dig in here to what the heck I'm talking about.

These other kinds of hunger can greatly affect your eating and food choices without your conscious awareness (until now). To break it down:

- **Sight hunger** is what food companies capitalize on with commercials, advertising, and marketing campaigns that display food looking so delicious you forgot it was a magazine page.

- **Smell hunger** hits you when you're walking in a mall and you smell cinnamon rolls or freshly-baked bread. You weren't technically hungry a minute ago, but now you feel your tummy rumbling. Know that feeling? Ever experience this? Those smells can actually cause you biologically to think you're hungry.

- **Mouth hunger** is that sensation of wanting something in your mouth. For some that might be chewing gum or craving the chewing sensation in your mouth regardless of actual hunger.

- **Emotional hunger** is a whole different animal. This is mainly the culprit of what trips me up. It's the difference between eating when I'm actually hungry and eating that has nothing to do with hunger. It's so helpful to know that you can teach yourself to stop, breathe, and check out what your hunger stats are. This doesn't cost a dime and has changed the trajectory for my overall health and relationship with food. Now mind you, I still find myself using food at times, be it smell hunger or emotional hunger. The difference today is that I'm in the driver's seat making that choice versus feeling like I had no choice.

Daily Magical Practices #3: Intentional Eating

Ready to try intuitive eating according to your body's natural hunger cues? Try using these eating tips:

1. Pause for 30 seconds before you dig in to say thanks for the food on your plate. Notice your energy level and that of the food you are about to eat. (Whole foods have more energy, or life force, than food from a box.)

2. Put down your fork after each bite. How did that feel? What did you notice?

3. Contemplate where all the components of your meal came from. For example, a farmer grew the vegetables you're eating, someone picked and shipped those vegetables to the grocery store, there was a fisherman who caught the salmon, and someone picked the apples. How does it feel to pause, acknowledge, and appreciate the source of your food?

4. Check in after a few bites. Where are you on the hunger scale of 1 – 10? How is your energy now, on an energy scale of 1 – 10 (with 1 being lethargic and 10 being super-energized)?

5. Wait 20 minutes before taking seconds or eating more than what is on your plate. What was it like to eat a meal with greater intention? Any new take-aways or *A-has*? How can you add intention to your meals going forward?

These are great ways to cultivate more attention to what you're eating and more awareness around your food-related habits. Once you practice these steps for a couple of weeks, mindful eating will become more natural. Each day choose at least one aspect of eating that you intend to be mindful about. This could be your food shopping, food preparation, or the actual eating. You might choose to make taking the first bite of dinner your mindful eating moment. Keep it as simple as needed to actually make it doable for YOU! *See the Personalized Body Nourishment Assessment bonus section in the appendix to heighten your food awareness.

Food, mood, and inflammation

Are you aware that humans have a subconscious food-mood relationship? If your attention to food and mood has been hiding in the attic, I'm inviting you to focus on your present feelings. The real deal is that different foods impact our body chemistry through the release of hormones, which in turn affect our mood.

While working on my master's degree in Health and Wellness Coaching, I also earned a concentration in Nutrition. I'll never forget during the first class when my professor Heidi Most explained that we have more sensory neurons in our gut than in our brain. Holy guacamole! (Avocados, by the way, are fantastic and scrumptious fats to ingest.) That tidbit of info she shared was insanely powerful, teaching me that our mind and body, or brain and gut, are incredibly linked. What we are eating is not just fueling our organs and giving our bodies energy, but it is also driving our hormones and chemicals that drastically affect how we feel.

There's also a deeper scientific understanding today around certain foods and how they cause inflammation. For me, eating anti-inflammatory foods played a star role in my life after I was diagnosed with Hashimoto's (an underactive thyroid) when I was 35 years old. Like diabetes, Crohn's, and arthritis, Hashimoto's is considered an autoimmune illness (or what I refer to as a condition I'm now grateful for). With any autoimmune challenge, studies show that eating foods that fuel inflammation, such as gluten, sugar, soy, or dairy, can exacerbate the illness and create more irritation in the body.

Just as I experienced positive results by eliminating inflammatory foods, many of my friends and colleagues who have experienced a similar health crisis have expressed that this has been true for them as well. Based on my experience, I'd highly suggest that if you have any kind of autoimmune condition, or even if you're curious to find out more, consider looking further into an autoimmune protocol (AIP). There are a ton of books, articles, and research linking the benefits of a focus on eating anti-inflammatory foods with your body's ability to heal itself. The most important mind shift for me was realizing that this is not a short-term diet, but rather a consistent lifestyle choice to help me stay healthy and well.

What this means, my beautiful friends, is that you will want to dedicate some self-research time to observe how YOU feel after you eat certain foods. Signs that a certain food may not be easily handled by your body include: bloating, cramping, rashes, tiredness, lethargy, gas, constipation, diarrhea, intense cravings, feeling heavy, and indigestion.

I'm not saying that you have to omit any particular foods from your food repertoire. It is your choice. You are entitled to your own choices about what you want to put in your body. Simply become more aware of the power your nutritional decisions have to affect your entire life. Your choices probably have a stronger correlation with how you feel than you may have previously believed. It isn't something that we are typically taught, so I am asking you to consider that it is possible that mood dips and emotional fluctuations in general can quite often be closely linked to what is on your fork.

The main life-changing ingredient to add to your well-being plan is always self-love and self-compassion. Talk about anti-inflammatory! Nourishing yourself with loving care, especially while eating your meals, can change the way you view your body and relationship to food.

Take the food assessment in the appendix "Bonus Section" to get more in tune with what makes you feel good physically. This is a tool to see what is working and not working for your body. We will also look at your emotions and how you react when eating certain foods. If you struggle with releasing extra weight, hang in there, as we'll dive into how your weight might be serving you.

Tuning into your body

When I started to really hone in on how I felt, I recognized that dairy made me feel nauseous and bloated. I had no idea because I was eating it all the time. For me, using it sparingly or not at all has made a huge impact on how I feel. I want you to start noticing how YOU feel after eating specific food items like fruit, veggies, dairy, and carbohydrates over the next three days. Listen to how your body responds. Remember, you are now acting as a scientist. Be curious and research what your body is saying. When I did this, I noticed after eating one or two bananas a day, I didn't like how I felt. But I do love how I feel after eating blueberries.

Notice how food feels in your stomach. It takes 20 minutes to digest your food, so watch your hunger level. There's no incorrect way to do this; it is simply taking an action and paying attention to the result. At first, maybe you notice that hunger to you feels like wanting to devour your entire fridge. Then you notice that after 25 minutes of eating you feel pretty darn satiated. If you want to simplify this process, pick a food group to focus on each week or every three days. Maybe you pick a day just to focus on hunger levels and how long it takes to go from hungry to nicely full.

This time you spend refining what foods work best for your body will give you incredible insights into the natural workings of your body. Pressing the pause button is a powerful tool to use not only with learning to eat mindfully and intuitively, but also with reacting to life and making more empowered choices.

The gifts of your life challenges

If you've been a champion at holding on to extra weight, I want you to consider that not releasing extra weight might be serving you. I believe we are able to release weight when we are ready to fully be vulnerable by loving and cherishing ourselves. My personal experience with myself and my clients is that holding on to extra weight often allows you to feel safe and secure, acting as a shield by protecting you from something you fear. We use it as a way to hide both from ourselves and from others. Releasing extra weight means allowing your body to attain its healthiest place. I'm not talking about letting go of extra weight to become skinny. Each body is beautiful and distinct. I mean letting go of weight to be your most healthy weight, whatever that is.

Along with the emotional protection, I believe there is also an energetic weight we carry as well. When life feels heavier, emotions carry more density, which can be a great reason to turn to food for comfort. It gives a respite from feeling emotions. The problem is that what we resist, persists. At some point you will be confronted with a similar unpleasant feeling, so the goal is to find other ways to cope without food. Before we look at coping without food, let's list all the gifts that using food and holding on to extra weight has served you. This might seem contradictory and almost absurd; however, we can't make positive changes without acceptance and compassion. The outer reflects the inner; they are inseparable. I was able to take off the extra weight only when I let go of my garbage thinking.

If releasing weight ain't your thang, substitute an area you want to change or share with a friend who might relate.

How has your extra weight or using food served you? *(For example, you might answer, "Food allows me to comfort myself," or "I don't have to be vulnerable in the dating scene," or "I don't have to worry about my friends feeling threatened by me.")*

Positively reframe one of your beliefs around your weight and relationship to food. *(Example: "In the past, my extra weight allowed me to feel safe in a chaotic home. Today, I'm free to choose to love and honor myself fully." Another example: "By carrying extra weight, I never had to worry about getting too much attention. Now I give myself all the love and attention I need and deserve.")*

To be completely transparent, I want to note here that I felt vulnerable writing this book as a first-time author. As I wrote this chapter, I noticed I ate a package of crackers to deal with rising feelings. No guilt allowed—only awareness that I was feeling vulnerable. I then paused, affirmed my higher purpose, and went back to writing. That, dear friends, is a miracle in my book!

Down with shame and guilt

Next, you want to thank your body for being of service in order to keep you protected and safe. You have done the best you could, and now you are ready and willing to create space for a change. Watch out for shame and guilt which can sabotage you. In order to move forward and make changes in your thought processes and honor who you are, you will have to tell shame and guilt to take a serious hike. They are dangerous leeches, and gone unnoticed, they will suck out self-love and compassion. At the same time, thank them since shame and guilt keep you comfy, cozy, and safe. They gave you the protection you thought you needed from an emotional situation. When you know better, you can choose better. I can assure you that life without them will be so much sweeter. Since they still pop up from time to time in my life, I have trained myself to say, "Thanks for sharing, Shame and Guilt. I appreciate ya both, but I am letting you go now."

Play with letting go of shame and guilt:

1. Where have I felt shame about my body or self? Where have I felt guilt around eating?

2. What were the gifts of shame and guilt? How were they serving me?

3. How are shame and guilt not serving me anymore?

4. What would it look like to let go of shame and guilt? Any resistance? It's ok if there is, as they have played a protective role.

5. What small actions can I start taking to release shame and guilt?

"The wanting more was really a desire to connect more with myself."
~Julie Reisler

Chapter 10 Tap-into-You Journal Space

This week try to be more playful with your journaling. Remember doodling, coloring, and drawing help you to tap into heightened creativity, intuition, and emotions. This is space for you to ponder how you like to play.

journal

TAP INTO YOU

space

"The thing that I am really hungry for is ..."

"There's no passion
to be found playing small—
in settling for a life
that is less than you are
capable of living."

~Nelson Mandela

Your Purpose and Passion

I believe we all have unique gifts to share, dreams to manifest, and a purpose that calls us from the depths of our soul. That's right, I'm talking to YOU, dear friend. Before you start considering how to change your habitual patterns, it's crucial to get clarity around what lights you up.

I'm inviting you to use the next set of questions and exercises to hone in on what truly makes you feel purposeful and passionate. Once you get a clear focus on how you want to show up in the world and what you're committed to, you can begin playing in the garden of your life to see what might need planting, tending, and weeding. These questions can be used to guide your personal, family, and career choices. Feel free to add other areas to focus on. The more you take time to zero in on what's important to you, the greater the likelihood you will be moved and inspired to take new actions and create change. Let's have fun digging together to see what shows up.

Here's another quote to get you going. I couldn't resist; I love this one!

"Chase down your passion like it's the last bus of the night."

–Terri Guillemets

Passion hunting

Now, it's time to uncover your passion. First, think back to when you were younger and what you loved to do with your free time.

For example, I remember drawing intricate pictures of trees, bunnies, butterflies, and cookies with a fine-tip Sharpie pen for eight hours straight, while James Taylor played in the background. Today, I paint quotes all over my house freehand. Even on my front door (Oops! I'm really not allowed to do that with our HOA!) and anywhere I can find blank walls that need inspiration.

What do you remember doing as child for hours on end?

Use the following questions to see where you are on the passion scale and how you can infuse those passions back into your life if they are missing.

Are you using any of these hobbies or passions today?

If so, where? How?

If not, why?

Is there a way to creatively add this to your life? What would that look like?

When will you start? *(Note: someday is not a day in the week.)*

I will start _____
By doing this first:

Then:

Do you see any correlations between your passions from your youth and how you live your life today?

If you are still doing similar activities or hobbies, how does that show up in your life today?

If you feel it's missing, where do you fall on the scale between 1-10? *(1 is completely void in your life and 10 is I'm totally doing this now.)*

This is a great opportunity to pause, reflect, and even write about ways to sprinkle back in some of the activities you loved as a child. For example, if you spent hours making up stories about being a spotted unicorn with laser powers in an enchanted forest, perhaps you might be missing some of that magical thinking. You may want to start writing short stories, drawing free flow, or even writing your own sci-fi/fantasy screenplay. Our childhood moments can often point to an area that's missing today.

Here are some more questions to ponder:

What would you do if you could do anything?

What is your most joyous motivation?

What activities would get you out of bed in the middle of the night to do for zero pay?

Not sure? No problem. This idea will eventually come. I believe we all have gifts and deep, meaningful, purposeful ventures to share with the world. You're on a fantastic treasure hunt to uncover your personal quest.

Try this: Imagine there is a compass inside your belly. As you look at it, you will see that there are different directions indicated like, "Being of service," "Teaching children," "Creating financial stability," "Adding beauty to the world." This is guidance about your area of strongest passion. What direction are you being pointed to? Take a deep breath, center yourself, and clear your mind. Gently see it, sense it, and listen for an answer. Then take note of what arises.

Don't judge or edit yourself. You're starting to awaken to what moves your beautiful, true self. You probably are getting a little warmer and clearer about what moves you. As a little girl, I loved listening to people talk and share about how they felt. I always envisioned myself helping others to accomplish their life goals. I was that kid who stayed at the dinner table way longer than expected to listen to my parents and their friends talk about their lives, goals, and experiences. I couldn't get enough of their sharing. Eventually, I got really good at hearing negative self-talk and started to get curious about how our attitudes, thoughts, and words create our life experience. Finally (in my late 30s, mind you), it became clear to me that I love guiding and coaching others to get unstuck. Nothing brings me more joy than empowering others to make new choices.

In order to do this, I must walk the talk. I know this sounds like a cliché, yet it is so true. Part of my purpose is to nurture myself with the utmost care and compassion. Self-compassion is not easy for a recovering people-pleaser like me. Self-compassion is hard for a people-pleaser because the focus is so concentrated on the outside self, on others. So, shining the light on yourself feels unnatural. Sometimes I struggle with this like a toddler who falls down repeatedly while learning to walk. Yet, each time I get up I am more committed to reflecting my purpose and passion in all that I do. Once YOU have clarity around your purpose, you will understand how crucial it is to your health, well-being, and ability to make a deep and lasting impact.

Passion is a big clue to finding your purpose. Passion gives you clarity around what lights you up. It's tied into your physical being. When you get lit up and take action, you light up your mind and body.

Now that you've dipped your toes into the pool of passion, it will be easier to see what purpose floats your boat. For example, my passion is to see your highest self and my purpose is to guide you to see it, feel it, breathe it, realize it, and become it.

Uncovering your purpose

Purpose is the big picture vision of what we bring to the world; our passions are the vehicles for the expression of purpose.

Earlier in this chapter you explored your passion(s). Let's review and write it down here:

We all have a purpose to love. The greater umbrella for human beings is the purpose to be more loving, compassionate, and kind. This is humanity's greater purpose. Finding your unique purpose will look different for everyone. For some, it might be under the rubric of love, kindness, and compassion but be expressed as a love for creativity, being an entrepreneur, an inventor, a mother, a pioneer, or an artist. Someone with a purpose of bringing beauty to the world might do that through their passion for gardening, interior design, or fashion. If you have a purpose of fostering and expressing love through family, naturally your passions would align to home life.

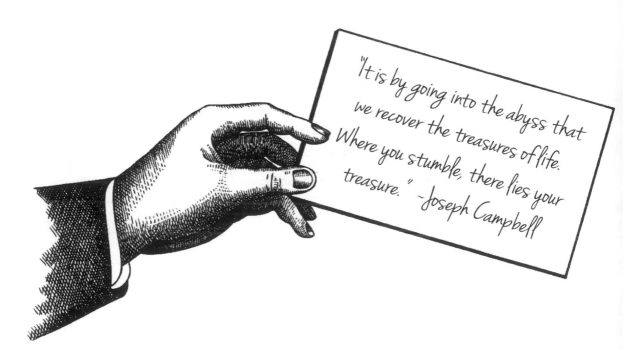

"It is by going into the abyss that we recover the treasures of life. Where you stumble, there lies your treasure." ~Joseph Campbell

Let's take a closer look to see what your purpose might be. You might already know it, and if so, that's great. If not, hang in there; it's still marinating and will be worth the patience. Personal purpose is about being in service of something greater than yourself. A great place to look for your purpose is your gifts and talents.

What are you better at than most? What comes naturally to you?

What would you do if you were fearless and had no boundaries?

If you had all the time in the world, what would you do? How would you fill your days?

If money were not an obstacle, what would you do/engage in/pursue?

What have you always enjoyed/been interested in?

What lights you up and makes you feel most engaged fully in life?

How would you begin to define your purpose? (key words, ideas, phrases)

Planting your purpose

Mother Nature constantly shows us how to live our best life. You do not have to be into gardening, tree hugging, or flowers to receive insights from nature about how to just BE on purpose. Naming your purpose is key to cultivating the garden that is your life.

Now that you're beginning to name your purpose, you might want to create a life purpose statement that will become your inner compass to steer you toward navigating your best life. Like me, you might choose to plant the purpose of being a role model for others. As I remain committed to my well-being and being my best self, I naturally inspire my family and others to do the same.

Whatever you plant will grow. It's easy to gloss over this statement, but I believe it is crucial to feel this at your core. What you focus on expands. Watch what you are planting and be sure it's what you want to bloom.

1. **Write your passion and purpose statement** and post it where you'll see it daily. *(You can use the template on page 161.)*

2. **Create a collage full of words, colors, images, or feelings that inspire you to be your best self.** Post your affirmations, purpose statement, and inspirational words where you will see them often (on your dashboard or your steering wheel to read while in traffic, not while driving; on your closet door; on your bathroom mirror). Make a date with yourself now. What will you use? What inspiration from your vision board will you integrate into your life?

3. What is the first thing you would like to do more often for a happier life? *(Example: I would like to cook vegan meatballs more often.)*

4. Make a note about how often you currently engage in this activity. *(Example: I cook vegan meatballs on a weekly basis.)*

5. What hobbies did you love when you were a kid? *(Refer to your answer from the Passion Hunting section above. Example: I loved to have all my friends over for dance parties and garden snack parties.)*

6. What do you feel are the primary reasons you are on the planet? *(Example: Being a great mother, wife, and loving friend. Helping others to live a healthier life by teaching them how to cook with whole ingredients.)*

7. How do you want to make a powerful difference?

Now, let's put it all together. Example: My passion is healthy living and cooking, gathering with my loved ones, and celebrating life. My purpose is to help others feel well, learn to eat better, and live a healthy lifestyle. I choose to make a powerful difference by eating and living well and inspiring others to find their healthy sweet spot.

Your turn:

The power of play

I have created the following equation (P5) to keep me grounded on my journey:

Passion + Purpose + Presence + Play = Powerful Possibility!

Feel free to put this in a place where you will see it often, like your steering wheel or your mirror. I would like to emphasize the importance of play in this equation. You owe it to yourself to joyfully play in order to allow your mind and body to relax, let go, dream, intuit, and commune with that playful part of yourself. I integrate play into my life by going to an arts and crafts store and coming up with hundreds of decorating ideas, or perusing small independent boutiques and finding new inspiration to play with. Another way to let my mind go out-of-the-box-happy is hanging in the produce section in Whole Foods. No joke—it's totally my happy place. I love being surrounded by fresh fruits and veggies because the colors are vibrant and it reminds me of the diversity of healthy nourishment in the world.

What are some ways you could free your mind from limits and add some fun? List them here:

Play helps me to restore my own internal balance and become more focused on my purpose. I see where my purpose intersects with play. We tend to lose the joy of play as adults when we get caught up in our to-do lists. When I'm coaching someone through a breakdown and they have an *A-ha!* moment, I'm immediately present to joy, excitement, and even play to some degree. As Joseph Campbell so brilliantly said, "Follow your bliss and the rest will take care of itself."

The important piece is to discover your personal path to bliss. I've included some more activities to help activate your child-like wonder as you further explore your purpose. No matter what you choose, I encourage you to select any activity or question with a willingness to be curious and to play. Our lives are a big classroom. It's up to us to start seeing all of life's experiences as learning opportunities.

More prompts for clarity about your playful self:

I would love to take the following class(es):

I would love to do more

The way I like to de-stress is

My favorite hobbies are

My favorite way to play as a child was

My favorite way to play as an adult is

If I were rating my use of play in everyday life on a scale of 1-10, where would I fall on the scale?

The play score I am shooting for is

What are three ways I can add more play to my daily and weekly schedule?

Composing your ingredients

Just like a delicious soup, you get to simmer in all the ingredients you've added to your concoction. Taking from all the nuggets of wisdom harvested in this chapter, let's serve your passion and purpose soup.

QUICK RECAP:

1. My passion is:

2. I'm naturally awesome at:

3. I feel most of service when:

4. My purpose is:

"There will never be another you. The planet desperately needs your unique purpose, passion, and presence." ~Julie Reisler

Chapter 11 Tap-into-You Journal Space

This week try to be more playful with your journaling. Remember doodling, coloring, and drawing help you to tap into heightened creativity, intuition, and emotions. This is space for you to ponder how you like to play.

"If I were my favorite animal, I would understand that my true purpose is to . . ."

"You wouldn't be able
to dream if you didn't have
the capacity to achieve it."

~Jack Canfield

Embracing the Fabulous YOU

It is my wish that this workbook has helped you to find your groove of discovering the fabulous YOU! My intention was to help guide you towards that sweet spot where self-love, growth, accountability, and bliss exist. This is just the beginning—personal growth is a lifelong process. Don't feel discouraged by that thought, because you are light-years ahead of where you were when you started. Imagine where you will be in a year or even ten years from now. The sky's the limit! Personally, I don't expect to ever "arrive"; however, it is clearer than ever that my present moments are filled with self-awareness—and they are a heck of a lot sweeter for it. I'm so grateful for the ability to both laugh with and at myself, while acknowledging my growth and progress.

Putting it all together

Change can feel overwhelming; I'm first to acknowledge that. Simply focusing on one step at a time on the path to your goal can do wonders for your perspective. It's like looking at a finished gourmet dinner. You might feel as though you'd never be able to create such a masterpiece by yourself. Yet, if you broke it down into steps, you'd see that first you'd need to create a shopping list, then to buy the ingredients, and then to follow the recipes. After cooking one dish at a time, before you know it, the meal you thought was impossible to tackle wasn't as difficult as you originally anticipated.

Be inspired by your bigger vision while zooming in on the individual steps. It is much easier to create small tasks that build from each other, eventually leading to your vision. It is my hope that during the time you dedicated thus far to working on YOU, you've realized that it can be a lot simpler when you break it down into easily digestible bites. All of the baby steps you've taken each day—journaling, awareness, and choosing differently—add up to significant and lasting changes. And the great news is that most of the time, if you have a goal but remain flexible about it, you may end up with something even better than you envisioned to begin with.

Practice, practice, practice

We are not meant to know everything; we are here to learn and grow. Sometimes we forget that it is supposed to be a fun journey! There is no shame in embracing whatever that means to you. In creating my workbook, I incorporated suggestions for brightly colored markers, sparkles, stickers, inspirational quotes, and all of the things that make me happy. The only aspect you have to remain vigilant about is practicing. It won't be second nature when you are first starting out. You will have to dedicate yourself to the practice of using positive words and sentences, sometimes catching yourself many times a day for a while. Not only is that more than okay, it is completely normal. With consistent time, attention, and action, your life can become anything you want it to be.

Acknowledging your progress

Let's start harvesting the bounty you've created throughout this workbook. (Notice I didn't give a timeframe. I know you did the best you could do and that IS more than good enough.) Envision us walking together through the stunning garden you've created. We are carrying a big ol' basket, ready to enjoy the splendor created from your intent, seed planting, and weeding. Notice the shifts and changes with some just sprouting while others are in full bloom. Consider each of these accomplishments to be a beautiful flower you can pick to create a fragrant bouquet. Or perhaps you were growing a raspberry bush and you now have the sweetest, most succulent raspberries. Go with whatever comes to mind. It's your garden...enjoy the beauty.

Any way that you choose to see it, remember the important part is to acknowledge yourself for all of the effort and changes you've made. I know firsthand that it is easy to overlook giving yourself credit where credit is due. My belief is that acknowledgment is crucial to your continued growth and development. Check out how children, and even adults, thrive with positive encouragement. This may seem a bit touchy-feely at first—it's all good. Even if it feels strange, please humor me and play along anyway.

Again, because this is your life and your dreams, you have the power to notice the good no matter how small. Let's find something that has improved in each of these areas of your life since beginning your study of YOU. Look at all the tiny details. Like the saying goes, "It's the little things that matter."

Where has my life taken a turn for the better?

FOR ME :
For example, I now meditate every morning for 5 minutes which has allowed me to do the following:
1.   To stop eating on first impulse
2.   Remain calmer with my children (i.e. not scream at them) and
3.   Handle road rage with grace

Your turn:

I now _____ *which has allowed me to do the following:*

1.

2.

3.

FOR MY RELATIONSHIPS :

For example, I am now able to listen better and communicate more clearly with my husband which has allowed me:

1. To have a ton more fun together
2. Less miscommunication
3. More intimacy ;)

Your turn:

I now _____ *which has allowed me to do the following:*

1.

2.

3.

FOR MY FAMILY:

For example, I am now able to respect and appreciate my mom exactly for who she is which has allowed me:

1. To enjoy hangin' with my mom
2. To stop judging her
3. To honor what she has to give (*crazy amounts of love and positivity delivered her own way*)

Your turn:

I now _____ *which has allowed me to do the following:*

1.

2.

3.

FOR MY CAREER :

For example, I am now able to have the confidence, conviction, and courage to leave a stable job and run my own business which has allowed me to:

1. Truly love what I do
2. Help others to create a life they love
3. Make a living from my passion and purpose

Your turn:

I now _____ which has allowed me to do the following:

1.

2.

3.

FOR MY HEALTH & WELL-BEING :

For example, I am now able to slow down, make time for self-care and meditation which has allowed me:

1. To be way more present with myself and others
2. To feel grounded, rested, and nourished
3. To have a lot more energy to do what I love

Your turn:

I now _____ which has allowed me to do the following:

1.

2.

3.

FOR MY FINANCES *(healthy changes in one area affect all areas of your life)*:

For example, I am now able to be accountable and track all of my personal and business finances which has allowed me:

1. To take full responsibility for how I'm spending and giving of my funds
2. To feel empowered around my finances
3. To be an adult with my financial decisions

Your turn:

I now _____ *which has allowed me to do the following:*

1.

2.

3.

FOR MY SPIRITUAL CONNECTION :

For example, I am now able to hear my inner voice speak to me and trust my intuition which has allowed me:

1.   To develop a rich relationship with myself and the divine
2.   Make great decisions based on my inner wisdom
3.   Feel more connected to something way bigger than myself and see everyone as a connected part of the whole

Your turn:

I now _____ *which has allowed me to do the following:*

1.

2.

3.

FOR MY SELF-LOVE :

For example, I now am able to own my sensuality and love my body just as it is (huge accomplishment) which has allowed me:

1.   To feel comfortable in my skin
2.   Not to worry or waste precious energy on how I look
3.   Be grateful for all the inner workings of my body and enjoy and appreciate my sexuality and sensuality

Your turn:

I now _____ *which has allowed me to do the following:*

1.

2.

3.

Where can I see new habit patterns?

How am I loving myself more?

What are my new insights about myself or my habits?

New dreams? *(Write them down. The more you allow yourself to dream, the more you will want to create. Remember, no dream is too big or too small.)*

How is my body speaking to me? What am I hearing?

What will I do differently now? Where and by when?

How has my "team" made a difference? What team would I like to now support?

Where am I still feeling stuck? *(Which, by the way, is totally cool. Remember, you are human. Perfection does not exist. Simply use this as a starting point to work through the workbook again.)*

Where have I experienced miracles?

How can I spread more love, joy, and goodness?

Chapter 12 Tap-into-You Journal Space

Journal about the changes that stand out the most for you from the work you've done here. What were some of your favorite A-ha! moments?

journal

TAP INTO YOU

space

"Having brought some new feelings to light,
I'm going to commit to reworking through this workbook again.
I will focus on creating . . ."

Embracing the Fabulous YOU

YOU are a smart, capable, creative, beautiful human being with all that you need to bring your dreams into reality! I love what Jack Canfield, co-author of *Chicken Soup for the Soul* said: "You wouldn't be able to dream if you didn't have the capacity to achieve it." Never feel discouraged because you don't know how to achieve your dreams. Instead, embrace the journey to getting there. I promise if you commit to opening yourself up, you will experience magic, meet so many wonderful people, and have a ton of fun along the way.

While you have completed this gigantic first step in the sacred study of YOU, I'd invite you to use this workbook again and again. We are meant to continually discover, learn, and grow through inner self-work. You have taken the very courageous step to wake up, look inside, and make the decision to create the life you want, designed completely by you. This is truly just the beginning and the best is yet to come, because the more you invest in yourself, the better your results will be.

I'm grateful beyond measure for your participation and willingness to hang in there even when it felt tough. By committing yourself to leaving no stone unturned, you will be giving yourself the most important gift there is to give—self-love. An amazing aspect of finally doing this for you is that it will continuously pay huge dividends into your own life, as well as the lives of all those lucky enough to come into contact with you.

Congratulations! Wishing you a continued blessed and delicious life. As always, I can't wait to hear about the rewards you are receiving for dedicating yourself to your personal development and embracing your best life!

With deep love, light, and appreciation of YOU,
~Julie

P.S. COMING SOON!

Take your PhD in YOU to your mastery level. Find out more about my online programs at
WWW.GETAPHDINYOU.COM/MASTERY

PhD in
YOU

CONGRATULATIONS

_____
Your Name

*You have taken the time, energy, and steps
to begin to see how incredible you are.
May you continue on your journey of self-
awareness, love, learning, growth, discovery,
fun, and empowerment.*

With love & joy,

Julie Reisler
_____

Having completed this workbook and taken the momentous step
to begin your journey of discovering self-love and embracing your dreams,
it is with immense gratitude that I award you a diploma for a PhD in YOU.
You are a superstar!

The YOU Contract

I _____, a precious, one-of-a-kind, incredible human being, promise to embrace my humanity to the best of my ability. I promise to show up for my life at all times. I know there will be moments and days where I have no desire to be present or engage in my current life situation. In these moments I will commit to honoring, caring, nurturing, and loving myself even more. I will not let one situation, experience, or limited thought get in my way. I agree to toss the word "perfect" out of the window, as I know it doesn't exist and will only keep me playing small.

As I start showing up for all of my life, my life will begin to open up, transform, and become outrageously delicious beyond my wildest imagination. With each experience, I am open to learning, growing, and gaining new perspectives.

I am willing and ready to take on the study and the wonder of me. I will be as serious and devoted to the study of me as I would in any graduate or certification program. I will devote the necessary time, intention, attention, and curiosity needed for me. I am open to life's abundance, gifts, insights, and joy so that I can unleash my best self. I am here, I am committed to taking action, and I'm game. I am willing to love and care for all of me — mind, body and spirit.

_____   _____
Name   Date

Have fun here, my friend.
Draw your own personalized logo or symbol:

Passion & Purpose Statement

Your Well-being Wheel

Rate where you are right now in your life for each category *(watch out for any judgment and compassionately let it go)*. Notice where you are on the well-being wheel and where you'd like to be. Use this wheel monthly, quarterly, or as often as you'd like as a way to visually check in with how you are designing and living your life. **Note: 1 = low, 10 = high**

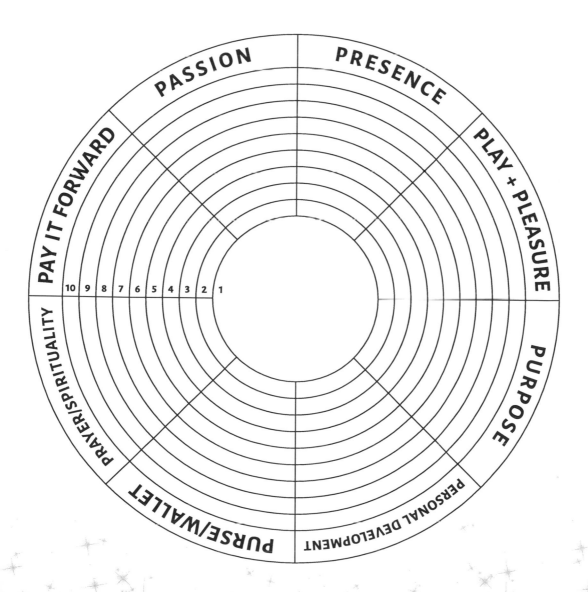

Your Personalized Body Nourishment Assessment

When I eat fruit, my body feels

Specific fruits that I like are

Specific fruits I don't like are

When I eat dairy, my body feels

Dairy items I like

Dairy items I don't like

When I eat veggies, my body feels

Veggies I like

Veggies I don't dig

How do I feel when I eat raw vs. cooked food?

When I eat meat, my body feels

When I eat carbohydrates, my body feels

When I eat packaged junk foods, I feel

When I eat whole grains, I feel

When I eat sugar, my body feels

When I eat . . .

. . . my body feels

When I eat . . .

. . . my body feels

When I eat . . .

. . . my body feels

Remember to pause and reflect after you eat. What are you becoming aware of?

Could you try asking yourself how you feel after you eat something for the next week?

Need extra support? Bring on your team. Find a friend or confidant who can help support you in your goals to better nourish your body.

Say Y.E.A. to the 3 Daily Magical Practices!

Y= YOU Declarations E=Eating Intentionally A= Affirmation through Celebration

Daily Magical Practice #1: YOU Declarations

It takes practice to get comfortable with really connecting to YOU and your love for your amazing self. I know this because I practice it daily. The more we invest in loving ourselves as our unique, authentic, and incredible selves, the more goodness we can give to one another and ultimately to our family, friends, communities, nations, and world.

Try at least one declaration every day, such as 'I believe in myself' or 'I am enough'. Pick and choose the declaration that resonates with you. Change it up so you are really hearing it and feeling it. Create declarations that speak to YOU.

Daily Magical Practice #2: Eating Intentionally

Ready to try intuitive eating according to your body's natural hunger cues? Wanting to have a better sense of what your body needs for optimal well-being? Try using these tips with at least one meal a day:

1. Pause and say thanks for what you are about to ingest

2. Notice your energy and hunger level before eating

3. Contemplate where all the components of your meal came from

4. Check in after a few bites. Where are you now on the hunger scale of 1–10 (1 being lethargic and 10 being super-energized).

5. Start a new relationship with nourishing your body, and being intentional with what and how you fuel your body.

Daily Magical Practice #3: Affirmation through Celebration

Each day you have reason to celebrate. Start a practice of celebrating YOU. Celebrate being alive, getting to know and love yourself, extending that love to others, receiving opportunities to learn and grow, and being present for the magic of life.

Please don't overlook this important daily practice; rejoice by injecting each day with the flavor of celebration and doing something kind for yourself. Celebration may be as simple using a joyous daily affirmation to set the tone of the day, doing something intentionally kind for others, and/or celebrating yourself. For instance:

1. Each morning say to yourself, "I celebrate YOU! I celebrate all that you are. I celebrate living as a reflection of wholeness."

2. Schedule a personal celebration!

3. Celebrate your connectedness

4. Start a celebration vision board showing gratitude

5. Celebrate play by making time for kid-like fun activities

> ## Y.E.A.!
>
> Saying YEA to these 3 daily magical practices will change the way you view, honor and take care of the most important person on the planet: YOU.

Guided Meditation for Self-Love and Inner Peace

1. Find a comfy place to sit (in your fave chair, on the floor [my favorite spot], or if you want, you can even lie down [although watch out for dozing off]. You can choose to time your meditation or just go sans timer. I'd recommend starting with 3 minutes, working your way to 5 and eventually 10 minutes; however, any amount of time sitting still and breathing is worthwhile.

2. Ground your feet (or bottom) to the earth. I like to imagine roots coming out of my feet spreading throughout the ground, reaching wide and far and getting deeper and more connected.

3. Sitting with a tall spine, shoulders down and chest relaxed, start to notice your breath. A trick I like to use is putting one hand on your heart (you can think of sending love to yourself) and the other on your belly (time to get comfortable letting your belly go—great practice for doing this). You'll want your hand on your belly to move in and out. Most of us breathe from our chests until we re-train ourselves to breathe from our diaphragm and belly.

4. Sitting peacefully and with ease, begin by inhaling for 2 counts and exhaling for 2 counts. When you inhale, you'll want your stomach to fill with air like a big balloon. On the exhale, let out your breath and imagine the balloon deflating. Your tummy will get full of air on the inhale and deflate with your exhale.

5. If you'd like, breathe in for 2 counts, hold for 2 counts, and let it out for 2 counts. This is a 2:2:2 ratio and easy to pick up.

6. Once you get still and in the flow of your breath, choose a word that fills you with peace and love. (*Note to you, dear reader: Your mind will have thoughts and jump all over the place. This is normal. You are human. Do not worry at all about this. I'd invite you to think about your thoughts like clouds passing through the sky. They eventually pass and all is well.*)

7. Allow yourself to feel what it would be like if your whole body were filled with this word; perhaps it's love, ease, joy, peace, grace, etc. Breathe this word in and out through your nose. As you exhale, let go of any negative thought, stress, worry, or concern.

8. Inhale the word intention (aim, focus) you've chosen and exhale anything that isn't that; anything that doesn't serve you.

9. When you feel ready, imagine the color you'd associate with this word. No judging allowed; just notice the color (or colors) you felt and chose. Breathe in this color and imagine your whole body filling with beautiful tones of this color. Perhaps you're noticing other colors entering your body, or sparkles, glitter, or even light. Trust that whatever you are picturing and thinking about is exactly right for your body and mind right now.

10. As you sit breathing with intention (i.e. meditating), allow yourself to feel supported by the ground and by the universe, and be your highest self. Before ending your meditation, focus on one area of life you are extremely grateful for. Allow that feeling of appreciation to take over your being. Perhaps the color and word you chose are also still swirling around. Enjoy the moment of deeper connection to yourself.

11. As you end your meditation, seal in your practice of connecting to yourself by taking three deep breaths in and out, taking your hands to your heart, and ending with repeating your word to yourself.

Enjoy the benefits of creating more space for inner peace; compassion for self and others; intuition; inner wisdom; and allowing your body to rest, recharge, and reboot. Feel free to add to this practice in any way you see fit. Remember, you are a gem that deserves lots of nourishment, care, and love.

Right Brain Mastery
Coloring Pages

PhD in YOU Community

Creating and Engaging Your Community Support System

The more value you add to your life, the more value you can add to others. You get to help spread the message that personal development and self-love are worth the time, effort, and energy. Your changes, shifts, transformation, and daily practice miracles can help and inspire others just starting out.

Research shows that you not only live longer with support and connection, but that you feel less pain and are able to better thrive. Get others in your life involved with what you're learning and taking on. As Gandhi says, "Be the change you wish to see in the world." My advice is never to go it alone. By now you've created a support team. Use your team! Designate that friend or family member, or even a new acquaintance committed to personal development, to be your accountability partner.

Monthly PhD in YOU Groups

Keep the learning going! This process is a lifelong journey. Gather other like-minded people who are interested and in action around self-awareness, and create a *PhD in YOU* study group to review the various chapters. You can discuss responses to the exercises, share your journaling prompts, or engage in mindful coloring together. You might do this as part of an already-established book club, too. Here are some guided questions to generate initial group interaction:

1. What were your 3 biggest take-aways from *Get a PhD in YOU*? Why? What are you committed to with these take-aways?
2. Which part of this book resonated the most strongly with you? Why?
3. Which exercises did you find fun? Which felt difficult?
4. Did you implement one of the Daily Magical Practices? Which one?
5. What affirmation did you create for yourself? Has it made a difference? How?
6. Are you taking more time to nourish and care for yourself? How?
7. How might you be a more authentic, more inspiring/positive, and empowered presence in the world? What would have to change for this to happen?
8. Is there something in *Get a PhD in YOU* that you are committed to trying for a month? Will you report back to the group?

Here's an example agenda that your group can follow:

- Group meditation (*can use guided meditation in Appendix 3*)
- Discussion about one or more of above questions
- Commit to the group one thing you will be in action around until the next meeting
- Creative activity (vision board, personal magic mirror, celebration activity)
- Close with creation of a group affirmation

Start a monthly Entrepreneur's PhD in YOU Mastermind, Women's PhD in YOU study group or a PhD in YOU - Magical Living group to track new behaviors and life events. For further camaraderie and ideas, go to **www.getaphdinyou.com/ community**.

PhD in YOU Global Community

We are all of one human family. There are so many of our sisters and brothers who feel isolated, alone in their negative beliefs, stuck, frustrated with their life, and desperate. They may not realize the importance and benefits of investing in themselves. Join the *PhD in YOU* Facebook community group to share what you are learning, to share what's making a difference in your life, and both to receive and give support. By sharing your new awarenesses, life changes, and stories, you will be empowering others to give themselves the greatest gift of all—time, attention, and intention to loving themselves more. **#getaphdinyou**

Continue your PhD in YOU Path of Learning

Wanting to take the mastery of YOU to your next level? Get ready to deep dive into *Get a PhD in YOU* with the online PhD in YOU Mastery course that will blow you (and your awareness) out of the water. Find out more at **www.getaphdinyou.com/mastery**

Giving Back

By paying it forward and sharing what you've learned with others not as fortunate or in the know about the benefits of personal development, you are helping to make a difference to the human race. Hold free *PhD in YOU* sessions or workshops in your secular and religious communities, schools, government, etc. Gift a book to those who can't afford it, and share how it has changed your life.

I believe this self-love will radiate beyond our comprehension and create a more loving planet. Who doesn't want that? Be part of the *PhD in YOU* movement and keep sharing your radiant self and how life is getting better and more miraculous. It is through our authentic sharing, vulnerability, and support that we can help ourselves and others to see that life can be a beautiful banquet filled with value, meaning, and happiness. Keep sharing the good, the struggles, and the life shifts on Facebook, other social media outlets, and at **www.getaphdinyou.com/community**.

PhD in YOU Resources That Have Inspired Me

TED Talks I'm in love with:

The Happiness Advantage
Shawn Achor

Your Body Language Shapes Who You Are
Amy Cuddy

Start With Why
Simon Sinek

The Power of Vulnerability
Brené Brown

Some of my fave books:

The Artist's Way
Julia Cameron

Miracle Morning
Hal Elrod

Loving Yourself To Great Health
Louise Hay

Mindset
Carol Dweck

Language and the Pursuit of Happiness
The Chalmer Brothers

The One Thing
Gary Keller

Thrive
Arianna Huffington

The Completion Process
Teal Swan

Illuminata
Marianne Williamson

Think and Grow Rich
Napoleon Hill

What I Know For Sure
Oprah Winfrey

Mindful Eating
Jan Chozen Bays

Mindless Eating
Brian Wozniak

Year of Yes
Shonda Rhimes

The Secret
Rhonda Byrne

Healing With Whole Foods
Paul Pitchford

Awesome Apps:

Mindfulness: Insight Timer

The Virtues Project Reflection Cards

Louise Hay's Healing Body

Transformational Personal Development Programs:

Get a PhD in YOU Mastery, The Online Course: An Honors Program in Honoring You (supplemental e-learning course)
www.getaphdinyou.com/mastery

Landmark Worldwide personal development programs (The Forum, The Advanced Course, Self Expression & Leadership program)

Any 12-step program

Abraham Hicks videos, workshops, and podcasts

Louise Hay || Hay House

Hal Elrod's Best Year Ever Blueprint Annual Live Event

The Completion Process with Teal Swan

Maryland University of Integrative Health Coaching, Nutrition and Yoga Therapy programs

Other:

MindBodyGreen daily blogs

The Huffington Post

The Illuminate Film Festival (socially conscious cinema)

Collective Evolution (the conscious living forum)

OMTimes Magazine & Radio (Powerful resources and forum to co-create a more conscious life)

Daily OM (Daily inspiration for conscious living)

Super Soul Sunday (The Oprah Winfrey network)

MarieTV (www.marieforleo.com)

Mama Gena's School of Womanly Arts

About the Author

Author and Life Designer™ Julie Reisler authentically shares the extensive personal-growth wisdom that came from her own struggles with body image, relationships, and feeling "not enough." Both passionate and compassionate, Julie reveals how she traded limited thinking and damaging habits for honoring and loving herself, and how others can do the same. Julie has a master's degree in coaching and more than twelve certifications around health and well-being. She is a mama of two, step-mama of one, happily remarried, and in love with her very imperfect life. For more info on Julie, go to **juliereisler.com**.

45142746R00103

Made in the USA
San Bernardino, CA
02 February 2017